Michelle Balogh is a freelance writer, illustrator, and passionate part-time receptionist. She holds a Bachelor of Arts in English and Music from UNSW, and in 2014 completed a Master of Arts in Creative Writing at UTS. Her work has been shortlisted for the Children's Book Council of Australia Aspiring Writers' Mentorship and the Scribe Non-fiction Prize. Following graduation, she pursued a brief career in beauty and lifestyle writing, before discovering that the stories she wanted to tell were closer to home.

HER KIND OF LUCK

MICHELLE BALOGH

First published in 2019 by Brio Books

ISBN 9781925589856 (print)
ISBN 9781925589863 (ebook)

Published in Australia and New Zealand by:

Brio Books, an imprint of Booktopia Group Ltd
Unit E1, 3-29 Birnie Avenue,
Lidcombe, NSW 2141, Australia
briobooks.com.au

Printed and bound in Australia by Ligare

booktopia.com.au

For Carmel, Marea, Margot and most of all,
for Shan-Yi.

Great-Grandmother

When the paramedics tried to remove Shan-Yi from her Bellevue Hill apartment, she flailed her arms and kicked and screamed. Unable to manage, they called a second ambulance for backup, gripping her knobbed hands in theirs. Eventually, her tiny, skeletal body was manoeuvred onto a stretcher and up the great spiral staircase that ran through the spine of the building.

It would be her last morning in the white art-deco cylinder, built into the steep hill like a lighthouse. My father was there that day, frantic, the paramedics trying to calm him too as they carried out Shan-Yi and loaded her into the ambulance. The nurses at the palliative care ward said that the arm flailing was typical—a sure sign that she'd be going soon. They were right. She lasted less than twenty-four hours.

I doubt she was sad to go. Shan-Yi had no fear of death—in fact, she'd been expecting it for years. Not because of illness or age, although she eventually suffered both, but because it had been foretold. It was the stuff of family folklore—words spoken by a mystic on a barren island decades before—that she would live to ninety. Throughout my childhood, Shan-Yi always spoke as though she expected to drop dead on her ninetieth birthday. I never asked exactly what she imagined would happen—one of a thousand unanswered questions that went with her when she died.

I was eighteen years old at Shan-Yi's ninetieth birthday party, six years earlier; a lavish dinner with guests from all over Sydney. My brother, Tristan, and I were the youngest at the table, seated in pride of place by her side, surrounded by second cousins twice removed—a Jewish–Hungarian patchwork of a family. Hers was the only Chinese face present, the matriarch dressed in her signature black and gold, accented with jade and pearls. As kids, we didn't entirely know how the rest of those faces related to us; all we knew was that Shan-Yi was our grandmother. *Great*-grandmother, she always reminded us—a title in which she took pride. If it bothered her that people might wonder how these pasty white kids came to have a Chinese great-grandmother she didn't let it show. *Step*-great-grandmother was never a term she used. Her husband, my great-grandfather Andrew 'Bandi' Balogh, died when we were small—in Australia, Shan-Yi was our closest family on my father's side. She was the only grandparent I had.

That night was the first time I noticed that her memory was starting to go. She may have lived six years longer, but she stopped being herself at ninety, so in that way the prophecy turned out to be true. I noticed her stumbling over words, but I wasted the chance to savour her conversation. It wasn't until years later that I started to investigate her lifeher life. To read letters and journals, to haunt libraries and museums, and travel the world in her shadow. At eighteen I couldn't know all the ways her life would change mine and never imagined a time when I would know her better than I did then, the familiar form of my grandmother, digging into dinner next to me at the table.

Although I'd known her all my life, I sat at her birthday party and made small talk in the reluctant way teenagers do, coming up with as many excuses as possible to go to the bathroom and check my phone. It wasn't that I didn't care, I just didn't know what to say. It never occurred to me to be curious. I was never a curious person until I finished school and was no longer forced to learn anything.

That's when I suddenly wanted to know everything.

Daughter

In the months leading up to Poon Wong's marriage in 1910, it seemed like the whole world revolved around her wedding. There were negotiations to be had, preparations to be made—family flocked around her, forming a cocoon. After so much anticipation, the rush of her wedding day left her stunned. It would be years before she would see her husband again. Lee Yee had left for America days after they married to live and work and provide for her from the opposite side of the ocean.

Friends and family seemed to adjust to her new life with ease. Lee Poon Wong. People she met used her new name as though it was the most natural thing in the world. Lee. She rolled the word back and forth over her tongue, trying to make it fit. The foreign scent of her husband on her skin and the traces of his presence in their home soon disappeared. Before long she stopped feeling like a wife at all. She was just a sixteen-year-old girl, going through the daily motions of life in her little railroad village in Toishan, in China's southern Guangdong Province.

Poon Wong became a mother almost as quickly as she became a wife. Her belly ballooned until her body was that of a stranger and before she had time to get used to the idea there was a fat baby girl swaddled in her arms. Perhaps it was because her husband was gone that she kept the child so close. The two became an instant pair—Poon Wong and Teu Ying.

Children grew up, men and women wed, men left China for America by the dozen. Villages across the Pearl River delta region were scarred by gaping man-shaped holes. Men whose fathers had left for *Gam Saan*—Gold Mountain—to work on the railroad, now followed their footsteps decades later, skirting severe exclusion laws to find work in America.

Teu Ying was six when her father came home for the first time. Poon Wong scrubbed her daughter's skin until it glowed pink and bright, clothed her in a brand-new dress and said, 'Stand up straight. You're going to meet your father.'

Yee could see immediately that his daughter was spoiled. His wife chased the girl around the village at Teu Ying's beck and call. He had to take control. The first time that Teu Ying disobeyed him, he sent her to bed without any dinner. Mother and child sobbed in unison, as though they were both his children.

*

For all the letters he'd sent to his wife while he was abroad, it wasn't until Yee was home that he described his plans in detail. Living in Washington state, he saw the way Americans flocked to Chinese herb doctors, eager to be cured by 'exotic' eastern wisdom. Determined to profit from this opportunity, Yee planned to study these popular remedies in Canton. Equipped with the finest training, he would return to the United States and open his own practice. He had already found a wonderful town in the northwest of the country where they would all live.

Poon Wong was proud of her husband's ambition. She noticed the way his eyes lit up with excitement for the future. This was a man who wanted the best for his family, who showed his love through the provision of comfort and safety. He was wise and pragmatic, a good father to Teu Ying. Poon Wong tried to imagine the towns and cities that Yee described and the life that they would share in the land of opportunity. But the images were fuzzy, her mind's eye failed to pull them into focus. She didn't know of any men who'd gone to America and succeeded in gaining entry for their wives and children.

'That's because their husbands are only labourers,' Yee explained. 'You'll be the wife and daughter of a merchant. The families of businessmen are welcome in America.'

Poon Wong had never seen an American. The thought of crossing the ocean scared her. Shame burned deep in her belly but as a good wife, she wanted her husband to succeed.

Yee left once more and a few months later, his second

daughter was born. He was planting daughters like hidden notes; reminders for Poon Wong that he had been home.

Now they were three. Poon Wong, Teu Ying and Shan-Yi.

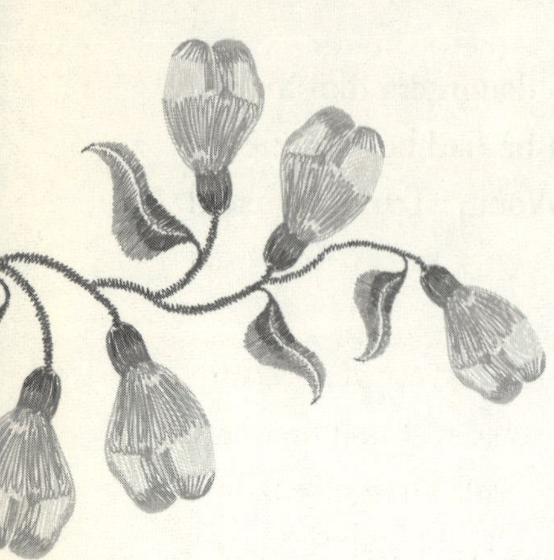

The Short Circuit

Shan-Yi died at a time when I wanted to die. We convened around her body at the Sacred Heart Hospice in Darlinghurst on a Wednesday night in July 2012. My father, my mother, my brother and I kept vigil over the woman with whom we shared no blood. Shan-Yi was so small in that bed. I cried, suddenly and out loud, but I'd already cried so much that year that it just felt like more salt—a ritual of tears rather than grief.

It's hard to explain how I came to feel that way. For most of 2012, I lay in bed each night wishing for no morning. The littlest tasks were excruciating; a stroll down the street to buy milk could result in a fit of inexplicable tears; the effort of rising and breathing and walking was enough to split me into pieces. I hadn't been to uni or work in ages—I didn't have the energy, and I was awful company, so I mostly made sure that nobody had to see me. I looked back on each of the days that passed and wasn't sure where they went—my sparse routine ate up hours as I moved through life in slow motion, like a fly stuck in honey, heaving to lift its legs. I was embarrassed by my inaction.

For all of my studies, I had spent the last six years stumbling around. That was part of the problem. I couldn't find my footing in the world. While my friends charged off into work as teachers and nurses and therapists, I was floundering trying to become a novelist or an artist. They made choices that led from one to the next, like concrete stepping stones, directing them forward. I made choices that turned in circles. The days blurred in a bright mess of train rides to the library and empty coffee cups and pencil shavings. The harder I tried, the more time passed, and the more I saw the self-indulgence of it all. The weight of time and money spent hung on me. I wondered if I had taken the wrong path. There was a boy too, as there often is. A boy who left and took all of my confidence with him.

Mostly, I think it was hardwired into me at birth—a short circuit that meant my happiness could flicker out at any moment, leaving me in the darkness. My brother, my father, even my great-grandfather Andrew were the same. I once heard a story that when he had his heart attack, Andrew wouldn't let Shan-Yi call an ambulance because he wanted to die. I'm not sure if that's true, but I do wonder how she felt being married to a man with depression. She was always so curt and matter-of-fact, always wanting to know 'why?'—it's hard to imagine her having the patience for a disease that knows no logic.

I'd arrived at a point where depression felt inevitable, as though it were an essential part of me. Now that I understood the disease, I could look back on my past experiences and see symptoms where before I had only seen sadness. My final years of high school, when I turned from bubbly teen to crying mess, unable to trust anyone. I could see the ways that mental illness contorted my thoughts and caused me to feel as though my peers hated me. Depression pushed me into real-life fights with enemies who only existed in my imagination.

Now the symptoms had come for me again. I'd taken to alternately counting out painkillers or toying with self-harm. I wanted to feel something, *anything* that would lessen the hurt. To focus on the puncture of a razor through my skin, in the hopes that this singular feeling could make everything else disappear. Then perhaps, one day, I could make myself disappear. I carried a penknife in my handbag as a safety blanket, I took comfort in the idea of medications that could make the body stop. It was only the thought of hurting my family that kept me from making destructive choices. While others took on challenges, clearing hurdles at work and in life and in love, the biggest obstacles that I faced on any given day were my emotions. It felt impossible to resist against the weight of so much feeling. I was caught in a constant battle with my mind—a battle that I was losing.

That year both Shan-Yi and I had been bedridden. She had more claim to the behaviour, being ninety-five years old and barely able to move—but my mother was caught between caring for each of us. As July turned to August we were both getting worse, slipping in sync towards an end.

Soon after Shan-Yi's death, my parents suggested I move into her apartment. It would be empty until the estate was settled, after that it would be sold and the revenue divided between her immediate descendants—Dad and his brother Charles. Dropping me in there was an obvious solution to a problem that seemed insoluble. My parents' last-ditch attempt at hoisting their twenty-four-year-old daughter back up into the land of the living. An alternative to the other option that had been on our minds, admission to an in-patient mental-health facility.

I was getting an incredible gift, one that I hadn't inherited and hadn't done anything to earn. The opportunism wasn't lost on me. I wondered what Shan-Yi would have thought of it, my moving into her home before her ashes had even been scattered. I clung to the idea that she loved me and that she was casting me a lifeline—but the truth was, she had no say in the matter.

Ocean-Dwellers

For three weeks in October of 1920, Poon Wong, Teu Ying and Shan-Yi lived aboard the RMS *Empress of Russia* on the Pacific Ocean, the world swaying around them like the hanging vines of a Banyan tree. But there were no trees to be seen, no break in the blue to remind them of home.

When Shan-Yi first saw the liner waiting for them at the wharf in Hong Kong, she wanted to run away, terrified of the towering metal monster. She writhed and wailed but was bound to her mother's back, her four-year-old body wrapped in cloth. She looked down at Teu Ying, seeking comfort, but her big sister held her mother's hand tightly, eyes to the ground as they mounted the gangway.

The ship cut through the ocean like a great steel whale, clouds billowing from its blow hole. They slept in a six-bunk cabin, the walls and floor cold and white. They were lucky, said her mother, they had the whole cabin to themselves. But Shan-Yi didn't feel lucky. Her stomach churned as she lay in bed, her thoughts wandering to the other side of the icy wall, to the unknowable blackness of the ocean. Sometimes her mother cried at night, just as she had during their final weeks in Toishan. Where were they going that scared her mother like that? Shan-Yi wished that she could silence her mother's tears, cover her eyes and find herself back home. She missed her grandparents and aunts and cousins and friends. She missed the steady ground, the feeling of mud between her toes.

In late October, the Lee family docked at the port of Victoria, on the southern end of Vancouver Island, in Canada. From there, they were ushered onto a smaller vessel to wind their way down Puget Sound to Seattle. From the deck of the new ship they could see land to the east and west. The air was ice cold, but Shan-Yi preferred the gusty deck to the dark cabin below. She drew comfort from the sight of solid ground—the horizon was a jagged line of white-capped mountains, rows of tall green firs at their feet.

They made friends with fellow passengers, the ship was full of their compatriots. Aiguo was on his second trip to the States. He bent over to speak with Teu Ying and Shan-Yi, lifted them up over the railings to search for whales and sea lions, described the glittering lights of Seattle, the stone buildings of Pioneer Square, the thirty-eight floors of Smith Tower. Pointing across the water, Aiguo explained how the rain turned into little white flakes as it fell from the sky, how the little white flakes settled on the mountains. Shan-Yi struggled to imagine water that could be scooped and thrown. But she didn't have to imagine for long, by the time they arrived in Seattle it was snowing.

When they disembarked, Poon Wong and her daughters were taken to the immigration building where they were held in quarantine. They slept in a big room with all the other Asian women, most of whom were also Chinese. White passengers slept on a different floor, men and women kept separate. Officers patrolled the halls, calling out the names of those who had been cleared to leave. Shan-Yi preferred life in the immigration building to life on the ocean—but her mother's brow grew more furrowed by the day and she was soon joined by other mothers in a chorus of sobs and sniffles.

In the crowded room, women passed the time with gossip and stories, filling the space with lightness. They peered out the windows and over the fence, to where they could see black- and white-skinned men working on Union Street. They made up stories about American families living in the towers that cluttered their view. But at night, the chatter grew dark and threatening, stories of women who never escaped the big brick building, who were sent back across the ocean.

They were served American food and the strange ingredients twisted their insides. Butter gnawed at the back of Shan-Yi's throat, so her mother sprinkled sugar and cinnamon on her bread instead. Although they were finally on land, they started counting the days all over again.

Shan-Yi was in America for forty days before she met her father for the first time. When the Lees were eventually allowed to leave, Yee came to meet them. For weeks Teu Ying had chattered about seeing her father again, weaving elaborate stories and describing what he was like—boasting to Shan-Yi about the time they'd spent together back in Toishan. But when Yee stretched out his arms and asked Teu Ying for a hug, she cried 'No!' and fled to the other side of the room.

'You've become an American father,' said Poon Wong. 'She's not used to hugging.'

'She'll be an American soon enough,' said Yee, turning instead to his younger daughter who was wrapped tight around her mother's calf. 'Let me meet my new daughter.'

Father swooped Shan-Yi up in his arms and held her to his chest.

'Welcome to America,' he said. 'Your name is Alice now. Your big sister is Marie.'

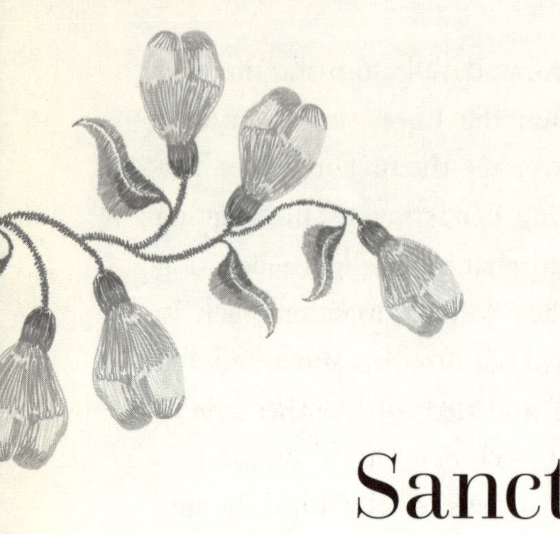

Sanctuary

The first thing I did was open the blinds, moving from one immense window pane to the next, flooding the living room with sunlight. A moment for the eyes to adjust and there it was: one hundred and eighty degrees of Sydney's glittering harbour. The blinds had been closed for years and I wondered how long it had been since Shan-Yi had actually seen the water. I couldn't remember having seen it before. Growing up, we always visited the apartment after dinner, eating at local restaurants with Shan-Yi and stopping by her apartment for coffee and dessert. In the window panes we could see our own reflections, a sea of darkness and distant lights. Now it was radiant blue, sailing boats, hills rolling down to the water, covered in houses, Shark Island, and on the other side of the harbour, the dense green of Taronga Zoo.

There was a little coffee table in the middle of the room,

round with four quarter-circle stools that fit under it. The surface was covered in carvings, protected by a sheet of glass—an elaborate scene of people bustling about a village in China. When we were little, my brother and I always sat at that table, perched on the child-sized stools.

At first glance, Shan-Yi's dark wood furniture—heavily carved and towering—all appeared to match. It wasn't until closer inspection that the forms began to separate—the cherubs and mermaids of the Hungarian dining table; the lions and dragons of the Chinese sideboard. The two cultures blended together in a shadowy mass of ornamentation, separated only by the olive green of velvet curtains, the burgundy of Persian rugs.

A wooden aquarium had been emptied of fish and filled with a collection of antique snuff bottles painted with miniature landscapes and tiny sculptures. A Buddha sat on a chess table, hand-painted plates stood on stands. The artworks lining the walls were labelled with gold plaques, 'Turner', 'Velasquez', and 'Rubens'. The decadence of the apartment in Sydney's luxurious Eastern Suburbs was a far cry from our home in the laid-back Inner West.

It was a forty-minute drive to her place back before there was a deep tunnel running under Sydney. In those days we had to drive *through* the city centre to get from west to east—Mum and Dad in front, Tristan and me in back, peering up at the lights and signs and skyscrapers. The journey was best at Christmas time, when the fairy lights were on parade and inflatable snowmen swayed in the warm wind; when fruit bats soared overhead and you could hear the cicadas chirping in Hyde Park. I loved that drive, I knew it by heart, and I experienced it with the wide-eyed delight of a tourist every single time. It wasn't just a drive to the other side of Sydney, it was a drive to the other side of my life.

I grew up in a universe divided by two. My mother was a country girl, raised on a cattle farm in northern New South Wales, the youngest of ten. I'd never lived on the land, but hers was the realm that I orbited in daily, a network of uncles and aunts and cousins, of dozens of kids lumped together, instant and irrevocable friends. We went to Catholic schools and were together for christenings and first communions and confirmations, for birthdays and Christmas and for no reason at all. It was a world of family potluck lunches, squeezed onto benches or sitting on the floor, of running in backyards and tearing through houses, of wanting nothing more than a frozen cordial ice block on a blistering summer's day.

My mother's childhood infiltrated mine and informed my every habit. When you're the youngest of ten you eat fast or you don't get seconds, you talk loudly and laugh louder and aren't concerned if you're rarely heard. I was the eldest of just two, but the lessons of big-family life on the farm were written in my blood. My mother, the athlete among her sisters, was always fighting to be picked first for a team in family games of rugby. Don't cry, take it on the chin, affection should always be communicated through well-intentioned mockery and jostling. Hers was a childhood of constant company, a hubbub of activity. My mother couldn't stand to be still or alone. So I never sat still, and I was never alone. She filled our days with outings and adventures, finger-painting and stories and train rides around town.

The flipside of my world was different. My father's childhood was rich in culture but sparse in characters. Matt, the little boy from Piazza Mattei, the square with the turtle fountain in central Rome—*La Fontana della Tartarughe.* The Hungarian-Australian-Italian child who read *Tin Tin* books in dim rooms clouded with cigarette smoke—who drew pictures and made models and played alone with toy cars. When his parents divorced, his mother and her boyfriend stole him away to Switzerland for high school. It was a swift move, changing everything overnight. Ten years later he fled his fractured childhood and flew to Australia, the country of his birth but a land he'd never known. Picking out a university near Sydney on the map, his European eyes miscalculated Australian distances—he chose the University of New England, six hours from the city.

The southern hemisphere Baloghs were the handful of Hungarians who lived in palatial houses in Sydney's Eastern Suburbs. They were a first- and second-generation migrant family, stitched together along extended threads—great uncles and cousins once or twice removed, holding each other close to create a community. It was a world of beach-front gardens and staircases that wove up and up through homes, a fascinating, expansive world—equal parts splendid and unnerving.

Dinners in the east were composed and quiet, tables were vast and laid with care. Brothers and sisters didn't yell over one another to be heard, greetings were more polite than effusive. When those same relatives crossed Sydney to visit us, I watched as their eyes scanned our house with bemused interest. Peering into my bedroom, I hoped I'd left it neat enough, my Barbies caught in a scrum of strewn arms and legs. I listened as they marvelled at the fact that we didn't have a dryer but relied on the hills hoist and expressed worry that we didn't have private health care. In my second world, where the houses looked different and the food tasted different, I was different too.

I spent much of my childhood glued to my mother's knee—freckled, limp-haired, and quiet. The explosion of eccentric energy that existed within me wasn't obvious at first glance. I was terrified of new faces and loathe to speak up. It took time for my personality to leak out around strangers, escaping over time in flickers and sparks until I was at ease. In my first world—my mother's world—I was already unleashed, comfortable in my role as the boisterous, excitable chatterbox. In my second world—my father's world—I kept the blaze dampened. Nervous to be exposed, I offered up little of myself.

That is, except around Shan-Yi. She was the constant presence at the heart of my father's world. Young for a great-grandmother, she was the same age as my maternal grandma and had the energy to keep up with us kids. She could be terse in her disapproval and always spoke her mind, but in Shan-Yi's home I was always free to roam—free to climb over furniture, to climb all over her.

When Dad moved to Australia as a student in the early eighties, his grandparents treated him like a son. Andrew and Shan-Yi were his home base in Sydney. From 1992, when Andrew died, it was just Shan-Yi—the Balogh family in Australia was a one-woman show. By the time I was twelve, she was the only living grandparent I had.

Visiting Shan-Yi was the ultimate in trans-Sydney travel. It was something more like international travel, or inter*stellar* travel. Her apartment didn't belong to Sydney, it didn't belong to Australia or to any other country. It was just like her—it belonged to the whole world. Sitting in the back seat, Tristan snoozing by my side, I was wide awake and ready to run down the spiral staircase and be ushered through her door.

When I was little, I was obsessed with the minutiae of the apartment. Probably because I *was* little, the furniture towering over me. The apartment was a childhood wonderland, home to an other-worldly grandmother, dark and at times even scary. But now that she was gone, the blinds were thrust wide open—now I looked down from above. As the sunlight revealed the thick layer of dust that coated everything, I realised there were bigger things that amazed me.

Shan-Yi's apartment was built for another time, an era of cocktail parties attended in swinging taffeta skirts and bow ties. When it came to the architecture, art deco was the order of the day and a curved alcove off the living room was home to a fully-stocked bar which could be revealed or concealed behind green velvet curtains. The doors from kitchen to living room swung both ways, enabling waiters to use their backs to glide through with trays full of canapes. There was a powder room for women to disappear into and gossip. I wondered if there was anything else like it in Sydney—a completely circular room, drowning in pink and furnished with nothing but an ottoman, an ornate sink and a collection of soaps and perfumes. The dressing room was a separate affair, a sixties luxe walk-in wardrobe the size of a small bedroom, with the kind of illuminated dressing table you see in old Hollywood movies. The bedrooms were lined floor to ceiling with bookshelves built into the walls and matching the dressing room, stocked with an extraordinary library of books.

I explored rooms that had never been my domain before. It was difficult to reconcile the dust and smells with the glamour of the apartment. I went from room to room with a bucket full of cleaning supplies, scrubbing and vacuuming and depositing scent diffusers. It was an apartment frozen in time—I had no desire to drag it into the twenty-first century, but I was determined to disinfect every nook and cranny. I cleaned until I was exhausted. We moved in my own bed, my things, but they were lost among Shan-Yi's.

You could barely tell that I was there.

Sunshine and Power

Spokane, the 'City of Sunshine and Power', was bursting upwards and outwards in the brightness of rural Washington state. But there was an order to its growth and pride in its planning. The city grew faster than a weed, but the parks were all plucked clean. Electric streetlights, installed in the business district, were like glowing beacons of the future—just another sign that the city had so much more to offer than any other around.

Yee Lee spent the years from 1910 to 1920 building a life for his family in Spokane, absorbing the industry and energy of the city and setting everything in place for the arrival of the wife and daughters he barely knew. He didn't work on a farm, in a mill, or at the brickworks, as most of the local men did, but he was just as dogged in his efforts as any of the local fathers. He learnt the restaurant industry and spent his nights in the steamy kitchens of Chinese Alley. He became a devout member of the Central Christian Church and pious families rallied around him, offering English lessons and assisting with arrangements to gain passage for his family. He observed these friends with a keen eye, adopting their quirks and habits. By the time Marie and Alice arrived, their father had absorbed much of the local culture and mannerisms.

Alice's Spokane revolved around home and stretched outward in straight lines, to school, to the grocery store, to church. The kitchen was the centre of her world. It was where her mother served *juk* before school, the thick rice porridge that started each day; and where her father brewed tonics for his store downstairs. The room was thick with smells of home—fragrant teas and fishy broths, a chain of dried tangerine peels hanging from the window. Yee darted from stove to benchtop, selecting chrysanthemum or willow bark from his shelves of jars. Alice watched in awe as her father mixed powerful concoctions like a wizard from one of her books. Yee taught his daughters how to identify 'hot' and 'cool' foods, to choose the right cooking methods to maintain internal balance. He soothed their aches and pains, fed them turtle jelly for healthy skin and ginger for an upset tummy.

Business was booming and Yee was always rushing. His clientele was mostly white men. Yee diagnosed their ailments with precision, reading their eyes and hands, then sent them home with bottles and jars and strict instructions for diet and recovery. There were two herbal doctors in town and Yee was always striving to be the best. There was competition in the air, a sense of urgency and excitement that thrilled Alice, even if she didn't know why. She smiled and greeted patients as they entered her father's practice, waved as familiar faces passed by on the street.

She wanted to help her father in the kitchen so she followed him about, jumping up and down to see across the counter, offering to stir and sift. She couldn't make magic the way he could—when her moment finally came she always made a mess. But Alice was not deterred. The next day, she would be there again—begging to help, eager to learn. She loved the tinkle of the bell as the door swung open and shut, the blur of new faces that passed through each day. This was her store; this was her home.

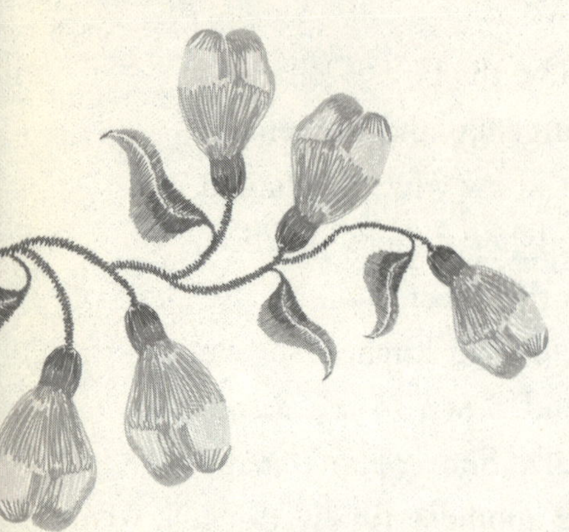

Son

'Yee Wo Chinese Medicine Co—our roots and herbs are the oldest cure in the world for all chronic troubles.' It wasn't long before Alice could read the words, her fingers tracing the golden letters painted on the shop window. While Marie would return from school weary and frustrated, Alice picked up English quickly. She learnt to read and brought books home from school, reciting stories to her father. At the grocery store she shopped on her mother's behalf, translating the cashier's words from English to Toishanese.

Alice liked the kindergarten classroom, a colourful space made entirely for children. While Marie attended school in China, Alice had been too young—now that she was old enough to go, she took delight in coming home with fresh knowledge each day. Alice's mind never drifted up the hall, to where her sister was seated in a classroom of children several years her junior. Marie's mind was full of maths and history that couldn't be shared—lessons from back home for which she couldn't find the words.

Women from church came over after school to help the Lee girls with their lessons, and eventually they were both caught up. Education was important to Yee—he kept a close eye on the girls' schooling. He was a loving father, but firm and observant. When it came time for Marie to start high school, he filled her head with ideas of college. It was never too early to start planning.

Yee's friends were a tight-knit community, men bonded close by joint experience.

'There's no point sending a daughter to college,' they said. 'Why pay to educate another man's wife?'

'Do you want to live in a world where only every second person has a good head on their shoulders?' asked Yee. 'My daughters are going to be intelligent women. They're going to have good jobs.'

Alice was only seven years old when Yee sought out a private violin teacher for his daughter. He wanted a well-rounded education for the girls and valued the skill of musicianship.

When her father insisted on daily practice, Alice applied herself dutifully. The violent squeak of the rented instrument drifted out the windows and down the street. She was banned from playing during business hours for fear of driving away customers—in the evenings she followed her father's instruction and worked hard at her music.

There were times when Alice resented the hours of

practice that could have been spent lazily reading a book. But as she grew older, the squeaks slowly began to morph into melodies.

Alice was six years younger than Marie and six years older than her baby sister, Cora. Her mother and father had been praying for a boy, but Alice was secretly pleased to have a little sister. Boys at school fought with sticks and pulled hair, they called her names she didn't dare repeat to her parents. She didn't need a boy in her home.

Despite Alice's distaste for boys, her parents' prayers were eventually answered. Two years after Cora's birth, David was born. For nine months, Yee showed off the baby—at church and at work he introduced his son with pride. Giggling and squirming in his high chair, David became the mascot of Yee Wo Chinese Medicine Co.

But nine months were all that David would see. When spinal meningitis came for his son, all of Yee's remedies failed him. At the hospital, doctors shook their heads and averted their gaze. The family of six spent days at David's sickbed, and then they became five once more.

Spokane's sunshine grew vulgar. The days were too bright, too garish for Yee. Customers continued to flock to his practice, but Yee saw pretence wherever he looked. A man who could not save his own son was no doctor. He sold his business and his home. There was no more hope to be mined in Spokane.

Girlfriend

Before long it almost felt normal to get ready in Shan-Yi's dressing room, to pass the harbour views on the way to the kitchen. I figured out how to use the rickety sixties' stove top, how to relight the hot-water system each time the gas went out. I slept with the curtains open, I could see the stars from my bed. In the morning, sunlight flooded the room and for the first time in a long time I started waking early.

My life existed in the cracks between hers. I could spend a whole day lost in her world, before a crumpled pair of jeans or a pile of dirty dishes drew me back down to Earth. As I moved between her possessions my mind wandered back and forward, across the decades of her life and through the twenty-four years of mine. It was an effort to root my thoughts in the present, to keep myself from reliving the past, recycling memories until they were worn as thin as the carpet.

Despite the new surroundings, I was stuck on three weeks in January—my last three weeks with Luke. There was the version of me that existed before then and the one that existed after. If I could be that girl—the January Michelle—I might just be able to move on and make something of my life. But I was too busy running conversations on repeat, binge-watching scenes until my eyes watered and my neck ached.

At the start of 2012, Luke was a big bear—a great warm chest that I could lean into. He was tall and strong, an anchor to keep me from running in a circle. Prickly and sensitive, his temper flared when I knocked against his soft spots—but his eyes were wide with laughter and kindness. It was easy to be around him and I wanted to hold him so tight that we would begin to meld together. Being part of a twosome made the future look bright.

We were friends from high school, but it wasn't until we were twenty-two that things changed between us. It was an easy transition—we only needed to take a few steps closer to shift into physical and emotional intimacy. Our relationship was a summer romance, of steamy evenings walking the streets of Strathfield; of spilling out of bars in the early morning, sweat dripping down our sides. We worked together at the Big Day Out, collecting tickets at the festival entrance to earn ourselves free access. As the day closed in we held each other close, rum and coke seeping from our pores while Noel Gallagher crooned 'Champagne Supernova'.

I didn't see the silence coming.

We had just returned from his brother's wedding in the

Hunter Valley. I enjoyed being introduced to his relatives, being shown off, his arm looped in mine. I imagined what it would be like to introduce him to Shan-Yi. It was everything I wanted—to have someone choose me. I was so busy leaning in that I never noticed him leaning away.

A couple of weeks later he became an alert on my phone. I spent hours waiting for the chime of a message, my days a series of anxious glances towards my handbag. I played the cool girl and tried not to push. Where I was warm and expressive, he was reticent and full of self-doubt. I knew that wanting him would make me ugly in his eyes, so I resisted every instinct, bottled up the feelings of hurt and neglect. When I finally cracked and texted, I hated myself for it. I hated myself for feeling too much. His reply came through in an instant, *'I wanted to see how long you could go without texting me.'*

Every time I felt anything at all, I became the person he said that I was. When I loved him, I was instantly disgusting—the cliché of a needy girl, simpering and sappy, besotted. When I hated him, I was a monster—causing drama, ruining the summer. I lurched back and forth, trying to fix our relationship, trying to be the girl that he had wanted to call his own.

The final blow came through Facebook, the night before Valentine's Day.

'I'm hoping if I ignore my girlfriend on Valentine's Day, she'll get the message and fuck off.'

His words were broadcast on a friend's wall. It was funny, really, what a good story it was—the perfect bad-breakup anecdote. I would have laughed if I hadn't been so broken.

That one sentence, typed into the deepest depths of my brain—that sentence along with all the ones that followed, the ones he rallied in defence.

'I didn't know you could see that.'

'You talk about the amazing times we had and I have no idea what you're talking about.'

'You're fucking crazy, nobody will ever want to be with you.'

Luke's words echoed around Shan-Yi's apartment and slotted between the books, gathering like dust among the ornaments. His words took the things that I knew and turned them upside down. The excitement and enthusiasm that made me fun to be around were frightening in their intensity. The passion and perseverance that saw me strive towards my goals were nothing but obsession and mania. The emotion that made me creative was concrete proof that I was crazy, that I would always be alone. Luke took the things that I liked about myself—the things in which I took comfort—and turned them into weapons. When he left, the weapons remained, gathering the strength to strike on their own. Now, they threatened to fill the apartment with darkness.

Cookies

With the business sold, Yee packed up his family and headed east towards New York City, driving across the country to start their brand-new life. It was the summer of 1926, and the three growing girls wriggled against one another in the back seat of the little Ford, all their precious possessions piled up between their legs.

'I'm hungry!' said Cora.

'I just gave you an apple,' said Poon Wong. 'Settle your sister, Marie.'

Sixteen-year-old Marie made a half-hearted attempt to hold the toddler still, but Cora broke free from her grasp, crawling over Alice to peer out the window. Yee was driving his family to New York, but not directly. They had been in America for six years and it was time that they explored some of the country. Alice wanted to see new things, but the idea of driving for days on end seemed like absolute madness. She folded her arms across her chest and stared at the back of her mother's neck, willing her mother to defy her father, to insist that they head directly to the east coast. But she knew that it was no use. Her mother always agreed with her father, no matter what he said. Alice closed her eyes and tried to fall asleep—they had only been travelling for a few hours.

Yee had been hearing about the Palouse country for years, a geographic wonder on the border of Idaho and Washington. But this was the first time he'd actually seen it. They were only a short distance southeast of Spokane, but the landscape had changed entirely. The hills were rippling like sand dunes out to the horizon. A grassy blanket of greens and brown, tossed out to dry in the July sun. He wanted to drive in circles, to point out every curve and crescent to his family. It had been months since he had felt this light. Feet on the pedals, engine roaring, there was a great country stretched out before him. Opportunity inflated his chest, just as it had when he first crossed the Pacific. The places behind him? They were growing further away by the minute.

They passed through a town less than one hundred miles from Spokane called Moscow. Alice stared out the window at the towering elevators of the flour mill on one side of the town and the green hills closing in on the other. They saw churches and a schoolyard, children spilling from the gates. She watched well-kept houses with emerald lawns glide by as her father drove towards the centre of the little community. Finally heeding their requests, Yee pulled up to the kerb to buy a snack for his daughters.

Poon Wong and her girls had been sitting in the parked car for fifteen minutes. The heat seemed to expand between them like a dense cloud. They waited for their snack and waited to get going, waited for the never-ending drive to recommence. Alice suspected that her father was less concerned with filling their stomachs than silencing them with full mouths. She gazed out the window—dignified stone storefronts were stacked one against the next in tidy rows, baking in the summer's haze. They were parked on the corner of Main and Third, the same names as streets she'd known back home in Spokane. She guessed they would see the same names all over America. She wondered why they couldn't come up with something more creative—Alice Street, perhaps. But as she looked down East Third Street she could see that although the names were the same, these streets were different. Spokane was more like a city whereas Moscow was just a town. She watched customers crossing the street, coming out of a bank and going into the café. 'Huff's Café' was spelled out in neon, 'The Moscow National Bank' was inscribed into a stone wall. She couldn't understand what was taking her father so long.

When Yee returned to the car he passed a bag of cookies to the girls.

'Where are we going now?' asked Alice.

'Nowhere,' said Yee. 'I just bought the café.'

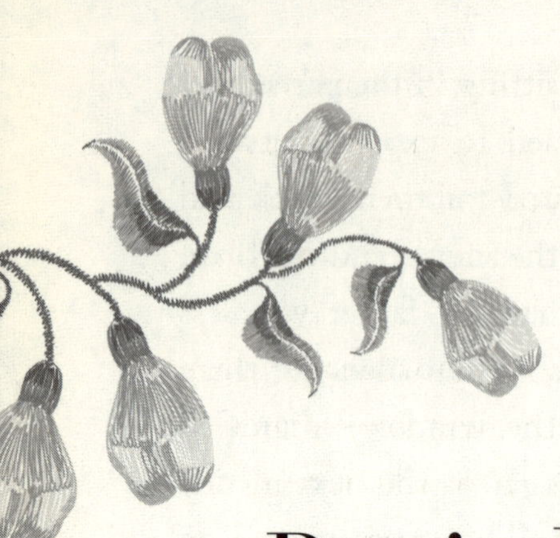

Buried Treasure

For a while I missed the hidden clues, the answers to questions that I never knew to ask. I was too busy fussing and cleaning; too distracted to search for buried treasure. I fitted my possessions around Shan-Yi's, only using a couple of rooms. It was as though I were house sitting, living tentatively so that everything would be just so when she eventually returned. But after a while, I started to dig in.

Kneeling on the hallway floor, I used a ruler to wedge open the curved door of a sideboard. It was the first time I had even noticed the door was there—the furniture was so heavily embellished that it was nearly impossible to tell where drawers opened and lids lifted. Swinging the door aside, I uncovered a collection of recording equipment, a portable radio, oversized headphones, and a cone-shaped microphone that looked like it had been around since the fifties. I couldn't imagine what Shan-Yi would have used all the technology for—I supposed these things must have been Andrew's, although I couldn't guess how they factored into his work as an importer. I had no way of finding out—I had never even known the man.

In one room, I uncovered a drawer full of aeroplane eye masks, another of soaps from international hotels, another of individually packaged toothpicks. It was as though my great-grandparents had been preparing for some sort of toiletry-specific trade embargo.

The deeper I dug, the more I found. Secrets and treasures that weren't just concealed by the sheer volume of possessions, but which had been hidden on purpose. Some bookshelves had false backs—panels that opened to reveal a cavity hiding a silver tea set or important files. Old books piled up on a cupboard proved to be hollow, concealing crystal shot glasses and a bottle of scotch. In a tiny ceramic saucepan, the size of a thimble, I found a message scrawled on a scrap of paper—'$5000 in white handbag'. I turned the dressing room upside down, but the white handbag was nowhere to be found.

There were hundreds of photo albums, filled with artworks in black and white. Shan-Yi in 1936, wrapped in a fur coat, silhouetted against the pale grey of the Taj Mahal. Hanging off a yacht in Sydney Harbour, hair braided like Heidi, smoking in a broad bamboo hat. Coquettish, posing in bed, a kimono draped over her chest, long black hair fanning across a pillow.

Then there was the paper—folded up with care or shoved aside, filed away in the study or hidden between cookbooks in the kitchen. There were drawers full of paper, shelves full of paper. I pulled a creased letter from the bedside cupboard, clearing out the space in an attempt to make way for my pyjamas. It was caught in piles of receipts and business correspondence, secured together with long-rusted paperclips that snapped in half when you tried to tug them off. According to the date at the top of the page—August 9, 1945—Shan-Yi would only have been twenty-eight. The letter was so vivid—chronicling a holiday in the countryside around Mount Stromlo near Canberra—that putting it aside felt like closing a good book. I could see the scene she described so clearly—sipping Ovaltine by the fire with friends and taking picnics by Cotter River with sandwiches and beer. I could see it so clearly, but I couldn't see it at all—who were these friends? What had drawn Shan-Yi there? The letter's author was so different from the woman I knew, the crumpled old grandma full of cynical words and a taste for the finer things in life—I wondered what she was like when she was just a few years older than me.

It felt good to disappear into her world, and each time I came up for air after digging through a drawer or leafing through a photo album, I felt a little better. I cried less often and I had more energy. I found myself becoming bored, growing restless—feelings I hadn't been capable of experiencing during the exhaustion of depression, back when the very fact of existing itself felt like running a perpetual marathon.

*

I had been living in Shan-Yi's apartment a couple of months before I regained a 'normal' level of energy. The move gave me an initial boost, but it took time before I was able to manage more than a couple of brief outings a day. At first it would be a quick trip to the shops and then, as weeks went by, I began to stop by the local Double Bay library to read or write. I fell in love with the repurposed nineteenth-century weatherboard building with stained glass windows that overlooked beautiful gardens and Seven Shillings Beach. Soon I was visiting several times a week, waiting out front at nine in the morning for the old wooden door to swing open, me and the collection of senior citizens who were there every day. I often went home to my parents' house in Summer Hill for dinner. My brother, Tristan, lived with friends in Newtown, so it was just the three of us. I was close to my parents, they always wanted to help, but the realities of mental illness forced them to sit in frustration. Their worried expressions stretched upwards into hope as I began to move and speak like my old self.

The more time passed, the more I wanted to get going. I wanted to make something of myself—to have a real reason to wake up in the mornings.

When Shan-Yi was my age she was charging across the globe.

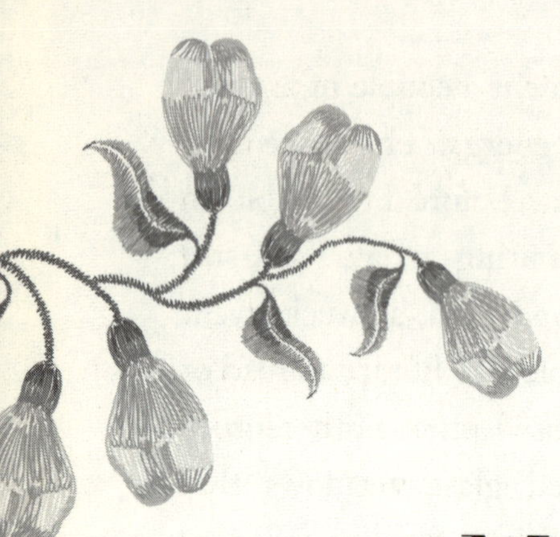

Moscow

Two thousand farmers and two thousand students, that was the population of Moscow, Idaho, the little college town on the Palouse. In 1926, Laurence Huff, the proprietor of Huff's Café, had just passed through the ranks of the University of Idaho. Like many UI men before him, he graduated with pomp and circumstance. He was going to go into business as a lawyer—if only he could make some money by selling his restaurant.

When Yee Lee wandered into Huff's Café and the two men got talking, Laurence was more than happy to make a deal on the spot. It was illegal for Chinese immigrants to own property, but Yee made an offer to lease the café and the Huff home, a weatherboard house on South Almon Street. Laurence Huff was on his way to being a lawyer and the Lees had a brand-new life.

Huff's Café became Lee's Café and life as restauranteurs kept the family busy from dawn to dusk. The girls started work, waitressing and hostessing. Every night they scrubbed down the wooden booths that lined one side of the café and polished the glass counter that ran along the other. Alice put in shifts before and after school, Marie walked from Moscow High to help out during her lunch hour. Only Cora was spared from helping out, still too small to see over the counter.

If they struggled to make the café a success, it wasn't for lack of trying. Customers in Moscow simply weren't the same as those back in Spokane. Pedestrians parted for the Lees, making way for this strange new family. Eyes ran over their faces, chasing them down the street. While there were other Chinese families, restaurants and stores in Spokane—in Moscow they were alone.

'This is going to work.' Yee was resolute. 'We'll sell bigger meals at better prices, open earlier and close later than any of the established restaurants in town.'

Their floors sparkled, their curtains were pressed, the countertops dusted every night. Yee took out an ad in the telephone directory—'Lee's Café, A Good Place to Eat, Booths for Ladies, 202 South Main Street'. They hired students from the university to work shifts as waitresses and an American chef to run the kitchen. The menu featured popular American dishes—steak, sandwiches, shrimp cocktail and salads—everything the locals had come to expect from a good old-fashioned eatery. They served potatoes every which way—French fried, hashed brown, au gratin, mashed, long and short string.

At first, customers turned up their noses at the Chinese

items on the menu—mushroom chow mein with almond rice; crab meat egg foo yong—but one bite at a time they began to experiment. Poon Wong spent hours preparing recipes from back home, the American chef helping to plate and finish them, making them presentable to the local palates. It was as though even the food itself needed to be translated to English—as though the Lees' faces, their presence in town, could only be understood once expressed by the local tongue. But eventually locals began to stop by the café *because* the menu was different. Lee's Café had something to offer that couldn't be found anywhere else.

When Yee first introduced his daughter to her violin teacher in Moscow, Alice had no idea that Professor Claus would change the course of her life—but she *did* know that she liked him. Carl Claus cared only for music, and that passion infected his students. Alice's teacher back in Spokane had been just that, but Professor Claus was a master.

A German immigrant, Professor Claus was a skilled violinist and conductor who had studied under the direction of some of the great musicians of Europe. When he was employed by the University of Idaho in 1922 as the director of the university orchestra, he embarked on the ambitious task of nurturing the group from an ensemble of ten students to a forty-two-piece symphony orchestra.

'We only admit the most technically skilled students,' he told the Lees, who planned to send Marie to the university. 'But we hope to have sixty members before too long.'

The university string quartet, which Professor Claus

founded and performed in, had become one of the most popular concert groups in the area, visiting towns across Idaho and Washington. Alice was just a casual student—what a privilege for a child to have Professor Claus' personal attention—but she arrived in Moscow just as the music department was beginning to gain a reputation on par with those of the leading schools in the country. Professor Claus had a keen eye for talent and he cared deeply about the success of his students. He immediately saw that four years of violin lessons in Spokane had fostered a talent in Alice that was rare amongst young violinists. With a combination of encouragement and discipline, he ignited a new focus in the young girl. Alice's sense of importance was boosted by having the director of the university orchestra as her personal teacher. From the moment the pair crossed paths, the violin stopped being an exercise—it became her life.

As Alice walked along the leafy avenues of the University of Idaho, students stared. She was eleven years old and she was Chinese, a double anomaly on campus. The crooked Camperdown elms bent down towards her like gnarled old witches, but she was not frightened. Neither the turning heads nor the scale of the campus fazed her. This place was her sanctuary. She made the journey to the music building twice a week in person, and many times more in her mind. Couples sank into farewell kisses on the verandah of Alpha Phi, but she never turned her head to spy what they were up to—her mind was busy with scales and intervals, the correct placement of bow to string. Arriving at the music annex she made a beeline towards Professor Claus' office, her bow in hand before she made it to the music stand.

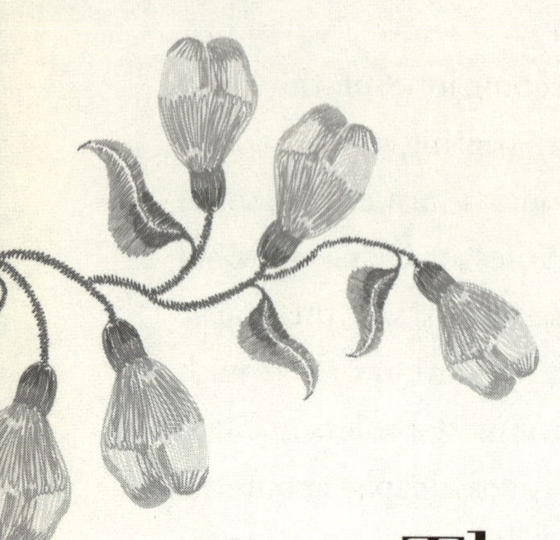

The Tower

The tower at Sydney's University of Technology is famous for being ugly. Down on Broadway, slotted between the latest in twenty-first century architecture and the classical sandstone of Central Station, the concrete block is a lone reminder of the sixties; an aesthetic misstep, the architectural equivalent to a bad haircut that never grew out. Students at UTS posted photos on social media, comparing the brutalist building to a Jenga tower or a cubic turd—but I liked it. I enjoyed getting lost around the inner-city campus—riding the old wooden escalators, reading in dark corners. In some way, the tower made me feel myself. UTS was where I learnt to love learning, so the ugliest building in Sydney would always be special to me.

I never wanted to go to university—I didn't spend my high-school years dreaming about further education. I was a believer in the Mandy Moore schedule of achievement—when

I was in primary school she was riding the success of her first hit single at just fifteen years old. By the time I was in my final years of high school, I was already running way behind that schedule. If I was to have a career as a singer or a writer or an artist, I would have to get started the moment I graduated, if not before.

I thought about things like that a lot—how to get where I wanted to go, what kind of person I wanted to be. I was transfixed by the American pop icons that saturated television and saw something more than just sugary music. I wanted to be someone like Christina Aguilera, who recorded the song 'I'm Ok' in just one take—lying on the floor, tears breaking into her ever-mighty voice. It was a song about domestic violence that I listened to on a loop in my early teens, a song that made me feel as though *I* was okay, even when my own home felt volatile and uncertain. My family, while bursting with love, didn't always act like those I saw on TV or in the homes of friends. Plates shattered, words designed to hurt. It was that song that made me realise what being an artist *truly* meant—helping people all over the world, people you've never even met.

Someone like Louisa May Alcott. I read *Little Women* hundreds of times over in the classroom library at St Patrick's Primary. My imagination lived in Concord, Massachusetts, where I sat in the attic with the March sisters, telling stories in their ivy-clad weatherboard home. When I sat down at the computer and told my mother I was going to write a book 'like *Little Women*', she said that stories like that 'came from real life'. Disheartened, I threw out my made-up tales of families full of sisters. But when I headed off to high school, I slipped the library copy of *Little Women* into my bag and took it with me.

I was obsessed with choir and debating and drama, with decorating birthday cakes and hand-illustrating cards. I threw themed surprise parties for friends, delivered cupcakes to their homes for Valentine's Day and sometimes for no reason at all. In high school I took it for granted that there was nothing I couldn't make, I took it for granted that I'd always be surrounded by friends. School Captain in primary school, House Captain in high school. Mates with the boys, best friends with the girls.

From the moment that I gazed up at an older cousin on the stage, when I was still in primary school, I was obsessed with starring in the high-school musical. I worked my way up the programme each year—from chorus girl to a small role, to a slightly bigger role—there was nothing I had ever wanted more. I was cast opposite my boyfriend in a production of *Disco Inferno*, but we dramatically broke up before show week. We stood, arms around one another on stage, singing 'If You Leave Me Now', staring tortured into one another's eyes. But all the teen angst in the world couldn't stand between me and my goals.

Shan-Yi came along to those musicals, sitting in the front row with my parents. Dad would drive her across Sydney to the big rented hall in Strathfield. Her passion for classical music never extended to disco or show tunes, but she clapped and smiled at all the right times. I don't remember if she had encouraging words for me, but I know that I wanted her to think that I was extraordinary. I doubt she ever saw in me the same drive that existed in her. Two sixteen-year-old girls, decades apart, but equally desperate to make something beautiful.

To say what I wanted out loud would be to risk embarrassment should my dreams never come to pass. Just as picking one single path—writing or drawing or music—would be to risk having the others fall away. It never occurred to me that choosing one direction might bring success sooner, instead I charged at every goal all at once, keeping a tight schedule. If I worked hard enough, I wouldn't have to choose—I could be everything.

Sometimes it seemed as if my childhood and teen years were a whirlwind of optimism and creativity. But it wasn't as simple as that. I was always trying to escape from my thoughts, hiding from monsters invented by my mind. At seven years old, the clouds stopped being just clouds—the sky was coming to get me. I developed a fear of rain so crippling that I was taken to the staff room whenever the sky grew dark, protected by the only room in the school without windows. I became obsessed with patterns in the sky, smatterings of cumulus and nimbostratus. I was a weather girl, a junior meteorologist, a dog with its ears peaked to the wind. I could tell when a storm was coming, hours ahead of its arrival. My stomach sunk, my hands grew sweaty, I wasn't listening to my teachers but pacing in circles, moving through a classroom without knowing where I was headed. I was crouched in a toilet cubicle with fingers in my ears so tight that sometimes I drew blood. It was years before the fear faded away—before the clouds began to sink back into the landscape.

There were other things—a classmate who cited a theory that a tidal wave would engulf the world in the year 2000.

After that, trips down the coast were met with tears and screaming. When I was thirteen years old, a plane hit a building in New York and in an instant the whole world changed forever. I made it through school on September twelfth, but I was back to my old staple—hiding in a bathroom, fingers shoved in my ears, blocking out the apocalyptic prophesising of teenage girls. I didn't go to school on the thirteenth. For years after that there was nothing that could strike fear through my heart like the sight of a plane gliding through a clear blue sky. I ran away from helicopters, I went into a blind panic at the sound of low-flying aircraft. At seventeen, I bolted from a picnic at the beach when a seaplane drew in to land.

Maybe it was just a glitch in my brain, a chemical imbalance that caused the side-effect of monsters under the bed. Maybe it was that things never quite felt stable—I wasn't always sure that I was safe, wasn't sure that my family was forever. But through dark times and through bright times, through boyfriends and parties and brand-new friendships, through phobias and panic attacks and domestic disagreements, my dreams stood strong. My determination never faltered—no matter what, I would get where I was going.

If anything, I figured that when I finished high school I would simply get to work—but success wasn't just waiting outside the gates of my Catholic girls' school. It wasn't enough to believe in myself, I needed an actual plan.

I was confronted with innumerable days to fill and I didn't know how to fill them. I didn't know *how* to be an artist; I didn't know *how* to make money from the things that I loved to do. The idea of going to university became a guidepost to steady myself against. At least one part of the plan was in place.

At the rolling green campus of the University of New South Wales in Randwick, I selected all of the creative courses. Music, theatre, film, visual arts, English—my days were full of songs and plays and paintings. But I felt untethered and lost. I wandered into vast lecture theatres and made friends with the students in neighbouring seats, only to lose them to the crowd of six thousand other students studying for a Bachelor of Arts. I was desperate to get going, but I simply couldn't figure out what I was supposed to do.

After university I turned myself inside out, writing and drawing from dawn to dusk. But if a crowded campus was lonely, my bedroom was even more so. The exchange rate of hard work for success wasn't paying off in the way that I thought it should. Nobody was counting the hours I spent bent over a desk or an easel. Nobody was interested in what I wanted from the world.

It wasn't long before I retreated to the community of graduate creative writing students at UTS. Classes were at night, so I was able to keep two part-time jobs during the day—working at the front desk of a city hotel and as a travelling auditioner for the Australian Youth Choir. My days were finally full, and my wandering gave way to walking forwards.

When I graduated for the second time, I was determined to work harder than ever. This time I would make it. I sent manuscripts to publishers, sold my illustrations at weekend markets. But when we broke up, Luke told me that I was doing nothing and his words stung with truth. I wanted to tell stories because I believed that they could help people, that they could reach into people's hearts and warm them from the inside out. But for all my high-minded talk, I wasn't helping anyone. As teachers and nurses and physiotherapists and administrators, my friends were helping others every single day—changing lives. I was talking about making a difference, but actually just sitting in my bedroom surrounded by paint, pages of type, and empty diet coke bottles. I had nothing to show for my time but an insurmountable HECS debt and stories that nobody wanted to hear.

Maybe that's why a single heartbreak could make me crumble so quickly. To feel lost and unwanted and without any purpose, to feel ugly in the eyes of others but most of all in my own. A broken heart and a broken life and a broken mind that combined to undo me—that was how I came to my year of sitting still.

But I couldn't sit still in Shan-Yi's apartment. Not surrounded by the memories of oceans crossed and countries travelled. Walking down the shadowy hallway, I felt more confused than ever before about who I was and where I was headed. But I knew that I had to go somewhere. UTS was where I felt steady and sure. I felt focused; as though I was working towards something. That ugly tower was my concrete sanctuary, right at the heart of the city. It was time I headed back there and made an appointment with the careers service.

Christmas

In winter, Moscow, Idaho disappeared beneath a blanket of snow. Families flocked to David's department store and emerged in thick new coats and fur-lined gloves. By day, locals shovelled and salted the streets, clearing safe passage for their children to walk to school. By night, the town was pitch black but for the blazing line of Main Street striking through its heart. The glow of lampposts and Christmas lights bounced off mounds of ploughed snow, slicing through the darkness of the town.

Thirteen-year-old Alice looked out over Main Street and the indistinct town beyond. The streets were silent; everyone tucked away at home. She could see a billboard poster stretched out over a vast brick wall—the image of a nativity scene, shepherds, wise men, and the Madonna bowed over her child in his bed of straw. It was Christmas Eve.

The Lees had moved to a new home—the house on the top of the hill—just in time for the birth of a son, Sammy. The three girls helped to look after their baby brother as the family prepared for the holiday. Poon Wong summoned Alice away from the window and back to the kitchen, where she and Marie were cooking dinner. The family had guests; there was plenty of work to be done.

The Lees were the only Chinese family who lived permanently in Moscow, but they sometimes encountered young Chinese men who travelled from their homeland to study at the university. In the neighbouring town of Pullman—home to Washington State University—there was also usually a handful of Chinese students. Whenever there was a holiday, Yee would invite all of the Chinese students nearby to celebrate with the Lees in their home. On Christmas Eve, the house on the corner of Jefferson and A was full—emitting a delicious scent and the sound of collective chatter. Alice made her way from room to room, hiding from her mother and making conversation with their guests.

Warsing Foo was different from the other young men who came to dine with the Lees. He wasn't Chinese, but Siamese and he wasn't a student as such—or at least, he hadn't come to Idaho to gain a diploma. He was more inclined to describe himself as a philosopher—a 'lover of knowledge'. Travelling the world visiting the best universities, he made his way through Europe and America, and all the way to the twin towns on the border of Washington and Idaho.

As much as her father valued education, Alice got the impression that Yee didn't like Warsing very much. She noticed the way he bit down on his lower lip as the young man gave a dinnertime lecture, describing foreign cities and cultures. She puzzled over what it was that irritated her father so much. As far as she could tell, Warsing was the kind of man that Yee admired most—intelligent, well educated, rich. He was everything the Lees were always working so hard to become.

But it wasn't Warsing's fine suits or the fact he spoke five languages that impressed Alice the most—it was that he loved music. Other than Professor Claus, Warsing was the first grown-up she had ever met who loved the violin as much as she did. He knew all her favourite composers, had heard symphonies by Beethoven and Paganini performed in the finest concert halls in Europe. Together they talked about the music they loved the most—he seemed to like it when she argued with him, defending her favourite composers. She enjoyed the attention, was thrilled to discuss music and art and literature with an adult who treated her as an equal.

In a letter he wrote two decades later, Warsing attested, 'I have never seen a prettier—more desirable creature—girl of thirteen, than Alice Virginia Lee in my full forty years of loving, wandering, and sinning. I don't expect to see one now or ever.'

When Alice performed for the family's guests on Christmas day, Warsing applauded the loudest. She watched in awe as he said to her father, 'Alice absolutely must pursue music, she could be the next Kreisler.' Alice's father frowned in reply—nobody came into the Lee house and told Yee what to do.

One afternoon, Warsing visited the Lees and found Alice in the living room ironing her father's shirts. She was humming the new sonata that Claus had added to her repertoire, pleased to have almost completed her weekly chores. It was an ordinary Friday afternoon. As soon as he entered the room, Warsing snatched the iron from her hand, looking down at the ironing board in horror. Alice's eyes darted about, searching for the source of his anger—but the linen wasn't burnt, the water hadn't been spilled.

His face was contorted as his eyes scanned her work. 'You shouldn't be doing this!' he snapped. 'You're absolutely wasted here.'

Warsing visited Professor Claus during one of Alice's lessons, and the pair discussed Alice's future. When they asked her to play, she was more than happy to oblige. Together they marvelled at her ability to conquer even the trickiest of melodies. She played with new fervour, encouraged by their praise. She swayed from side to side, her back arched, she felt herself beginning to put on a show. The faces of the two men multiplied in her imagination, until there were hundreds of faces before her. A huge crowd of fans applauded as she brought her performance to a close.

'France,' said Warsing. 'That's the place for you.'

Guidance

I looked around the office as the counsellor read my résumé, his bald patch lowered towards me. The room was small, the desk was crowded with forms and flyers: 'Surviving your job search', 'Keep calm and choose a career'.

My résumé was like a street-map of my wandering years. Part-time work at a bookstore and as a receptionist at a real estate agency. Full-time waitressing at the café down the street in the summer after high school. Debating coach, administrative assistant, freelance writer. All the lives I had already lived, all the ways I'd tried to fund the time to write and draw.

'We can help you tidy this up,' he said, setting the document down before me. 'Make an appointment for an evaluation and we'll go through it in detail. I'd suggest changing the order and bringing your most relevant experience to the top of the page. Highlight your achievements within past roles rather than just listing responsibilities.'

'That would be great, thank you so much,' I said, tucking the résumé into my bag. 'I need a job as soon as possible.'

'In terms of employment, your best prospects will be in reception and administrative roles—that's where you have the most experience. Once we've polished your résumé it should be easy for you to find work in the corporate sector. Is that what you want?'

It wasn't, but I needed money, and fast, so I supposed that it would do. I had come to see him for something else; I wanted this stranger to tell me what I was supposed to do with the rest of my life.

'Yes,' I said. 'Honestly, I'll take whatever I can get.' I paused, searching his casual expression, trying to find the words to explain truly what I needed. 'I'd like to do something different in the long term, though.'

'Were you thinking of something specific?'

'I always thought that I wanted to be a novelist,' I said. 'But honestly, sitting at home all the time writing was making me really depressed. I don't think living your dream is supposed to make you feel suicidal.'

I laughed to put the counsellor at ease. To prove that I wasn't a nut job, to show that I was joking. He didn't need to know that I wasn't.

'I was doing some illustration work, but I wasn't making enough money to live on. I'd prefer to do something creative, but I want a full-time job with a team. I just don't want to spend any more time at home alone.'

*

Sitting at a bay of computers, I completed an online quiz. I worked my way through page after page of questions, picking one industry over another—all the while wondering what my answers said about me. Agriculture over engineering, photography over botany, chemistry over electronics. Would I prefer to give advice about jobs or act in a play? Supervise others or help families with problems? As I tried to dig down inside and ask myself whether I cared about plants more than sea-life, I wasn't even sure what my honest answers were.

When the results popped up in front of me I knew that they were accurate, even though I couldn't figure out how on Earth they were determined. My top three careers—journalist or editor, teacher, and art therapist—one, two, three. That seemed right, even though none of those featured on the list of goals I had actually been working towards. If it wasn't for the feeling of giving up on the path that I started out on, I *would* be happy doing those jobs. But if I wanted to be a teacher or a therapist, I would have to go back to uni all over again. Maybe I *could* be a journalist, maybe I would work at a paper or a magazine. I could see myself in a job like that.

It was dark by the time I left campus. On the bus ride home I talked to Mum on the phone, recounting my experience and allowing little sparks of optimism to flicker through my voice. My bag was full with print-outs and flyers—lists of publications offering internships and tips for the perfect cover letter. I was carrying the instructions for a brand new existence—all the guidance I needed to start over. There was a sense of hope in the generic forms, a sense of opportunity to be mined from the handfuls of paper. I wanted to make something of myself, I wanted to build a life. And for the first time in recent memory, I thought perhaps I could.

Moscow High

Alice was at the centre of the crowd without being part of it at all. She was secretary of her freshman class and gave violin recitals at school assemblies. She was resident features writer for the school newspaper, *The Wocsomian*, and competed against Mable King for the title of fastest typist in school. But it didn't matter how much she did, she was always separate from her peers in the class of 1932. She was involved in everything and nothing at all, as though her years at Moscow High were just a play that she was watching.

When she wrote articles, Alice felt as though she was making up stories, describing a strange and foreign world. She wrote about the Signa Club Carnival, reported on the laughter, the spinning wheels, and the taste of hotdogs. For the 'Society' section, she wrote about a slumber party, noting that lunch had been served at midnight, and that a delicious breakfast had been made 'southern style'. She recounted all of the parties to which she hadn't been invited, all of the dances to which she'd never had a date. She was a master of words, painting vivid pictures of everything she imagined high-school life to be. Try as she might, she couldn't write her way into their world; she couldn't write herself friendships that didn't exist.

It wasn't that her classmates didn't like her, it wasn't that she was bullied. If anything, that would have been simpler—having somebody to blame. Instead, everyone knew who she was. They thought that she was smart and capable, they knew that she was a whiz on the violin. The other girls were always friendly, they greeted her with a smile and asked her how she was. They were happy to sit next to her in class and chat, happy to work with her on projects and share their notes. But she wasn't included in their most intimate conversations, she wasn't one of their girlfriends. She didn't look like them, so they figured she wasn't like them. With each whispered exchange, they built the wall up higher.

The boys, on the other hand, never failed to pay her compliments; it was commonly held that Alice Lee was beautiful. They told her that her eyes were lovely, her skin like porcelain, her hair like silk. They looked at her like an exotic bird that had flown into the school and landed among the pigeons—magical in its otherness. Their eyes followed her down the halls, making her feel as if she'd forgotten her clothes. She tried to hide from their gaze, to slide out of their pathway. Betty Carlson said that she ought to be flattered to have the boys talk about her that way. But Alice was never asked on a date, never asked to dance.

She watched her classmates tiptoe around one another. She watched them recede to their respective corners and whisper with their friends. She saw the outline of courtship but not its substance; she knew there were things that she didn't understand. Her mind raced with questions, but there was nobody to ask. There was nobody at home or school who would take her into their confidence. So she continued to live on the outside—the watcher and the writer.

She knew there was a world where she could belong, she knew there was a place for people like her. Perhaps the concert halls of Europe; rooms that she'd only ever imagined, but which felt more like home than the classrooms in which she passed her days. She felt most herself when she worked with Professor Claus, she felt most at ease with her violin in hand. The instrument was an extension of herself, her key to another world—*her* world. She looked down the school halls and out into the open, right past her peers and off into the future. High school was only for now.

Warsing sent her letters and parcels, gifts without occasion. His letters were full of artistic musings and descriptions of far-off places. When she arrived at the café after school, the mail would be waiting, green-eyed sisters looking on as she tore open envelopes. When she received a beautiful mahogany metronome, she wrote Warsing a poem in thanks. She told him which pieces she was working on with Professor Claus, kept him up to date with news of the family. Her father had bought a new restaurant, The Grill, and another baby boy had been born. It was difficult enough practising with six-year-old Cora under foot—now she had not one, but two baby brothers to contend with. She bemoaned Sammy and Bob's constant tears; her mother's banishing her rehearsal to the porch.

The violin wasn't the only instrument over which Alice laboured. She spent night after night at the typewriter. Aside from her correspondence with Warsing, she wrote stories and poems, letters to friends in Spokane. She kept copies and folded them into diaries, made notes of the things that she thought and felt and saw. Just like the articles she wrote for *The Wocsomian*, her uneventful life was reported on with care, her little world filed for another day. Late into the night she could be heard tapping away on her father's machine. Upstairs in their beds, her brothers and sisters fell asleep to the sound—the steady drumming lured them into dreams.

One afternoon, Yee was nearby when Alice opened a letter from Warsing. It was one of those rare occasions when her father wasn't busy with work or church or the babies. He insisted on reading the letter, on seeing what this man was writing to his daughter. When he finished reading he threw the letter away and forbade her from corresponding with Warsing.

Alice was bewildered. It was her father who had introduced her to Warsing in the first place. His letters were full of compliments and kindness, nothing to make her father angry. She protested against the ban, but Yee would not be swayed. There was to be absolutely no more contact between Alice and Warsing Foo.

Sister

Marie was better at fitting in than Alice. Serious about her studies, she headed off to college—by the time her little sister joined the freshman class at Moscow High, Marie was already a student at the University of Idaho. Alice looked up at her big sister in awe, the way she seemed to glide forward into adulthood. Where Alice was confident and opinionated, Marie was shy, but somehow, she always seemed part of the community, with a small group of close friends, always knowing what to do.

Marie was studying for a degree in home economics—a smart choice, she said; she could become a teacher, or use the skills as a homemaker. Either way she would be prepared. Alice admired her sister's pragmatism—Marie always pursued the sensible thing—not because she should, but because she wanted to. Alice couldn't help but be contrarian, she instinctively lurched away from anything she was told to be or do. Wanting the sensible thing carved out a place for Marie in Moscow. Even though she looked different, she could live like everyone else.

Alice was excited to join Miss Jensen's home economics class at Moscow High, but the realities of the classroom didn't quite meet her expectations. She enjoyed cooking hot lunches to sell in the cafeteria and she liked feeding her classmates, turning her work into a communal profit. She excelled at sewing and embroidery; her fingers were nimble and quick.

When the class hosted a Christmas lunch for their mothers in the school hall, Alice performed as part of an instrumental trio. Poon Wong flushed with pride as the other mothers stood to applaud. But when the girls returned to the classroom with its stoves and ironing boards, tea towels and tablecloths, Warsing's words came back to Alice: 'You shouldn't be doing this! You're absolutely wasted here.'

Marie joined the Cosmopolitan Club, a group of international students at the university. They went to the cinemas in Moscow and neighbouring Pullman, held picnics and attended football games. In Spokane the cinemas were racially segregated, but in Moscow and in Pullman they were able to mix freely into the audience. Through the club, Marie became friends with Mi Lew, a civil engineering student at Washington State University. When Mi graduated and returned to China, Marie thought she would never see him again. But a year later he was back, and the pair began to date.

The first time Mi was a guest in the Lee home, the dinner table was set with care. Poon Wong scooped great piles of chicken, vegetables and rice onto Mi's plate, Yee greeted him with a shake of the hand, Alice and eight-year-old Cora looked him up and down. Marie sat by his side—her gaze drifted to her lap in embarrassment but she smiled whenever he spoke.

'I'd like to hear how things have changed,' said Yee. 'It's been over ten years since I was last in China.'

'I've been in Washington since I was small,' Mi replied. 'I can hardly remember the years before I came to America, but I'll tell you what I saw.'

'I've never been to China,' Cora interrupted, her eight-year-old mouth full of steamed chicken.

'It's beautiful,' said Mi, smiling at the girl. 'But the poor are very poor. The streets in Canton were full of beggars, you're lucky to live here in Moscow, where all the children have a full belly.'

'A graduate of an American university should find good work in China,' said Yee. 'I'm surprised that you wanted to return. Americans won't hire Chinese engineers.'

'I hoped to work on the new bridge over the Pearl River,' said Mi. 'I made good contacts—I have friends in civil service—but you can feel war coming. It's no time to construct roads and buildings. Jobs are hard to come by.'

'How can you *feel* war?' Alice asked, sceptical.

'There's tension in the air,' Mi answered patiently. 'The government is worried that Japan will attack Manchuria. They send out pamphlets explaining what to do in case of an air raid, where to run and how to hide. Of course, the poor can't read the pamphlets.'

Mi smiled at Marie, enjoying the chance to share his experiences. 'It's no place to start a family.'

Alice stood in the front row of the church when Marie Lee became Marie Lew, a year after Mi's return from China. She liked Mi, he was friendly and kind, an easy addition to the family. Holding her baby brother Bob in her arms, she watched her sister become a wife, and felt herself transitioning into the role of eldest Lee child. She stood a little taller in her freshly-pressed cotton dress.

If it was hard to imagine Marie having children, it was even harder for Alice to imagine that she might be next. Alice wondered where and when her own wedding would take place. What kind of man would choose to make her his bride? The more she tried to place herself in Marie's shoes, the more she felt like they wouldn't fit.

The Crowd

I wanted to show Shan-Yi's apartment to everyone that I had ever met. And everyone that *they* had ever met. I wanted to make use of the space, to return it to the glittering society rendezvous that it was always meant to be. But it wasn't easy. I had been hiding from my friends—avoiding calls, dodging invitations. Resuscitating my social life would require the use of muscle groups that hadn't been worked all year.

The crowd was always the same people, assembling in the same kinds of places. We were students and backpackers and baby professionals—limping into adulthood through the hazy glow of an Instagram filter. Late nights spent at neighbourhood pubs, where local beers were on tap and cocktails came in mason jars. Everyone was thrifty—those who were lucky enough to be out of debt were saving as much as they could—so we followed the happy hours, ate corner-store kebabs for dinner. I may have become a resident of the posh Eastern Suburbs, but most of my friends were from high school and we were all born and bred in the Inner West. The pubs of Newtown and Stanmore were our regular stomping ground, most of my friends lived in share houses nearby.

Even before depression, it was easy to grow disillusioned with the sameness of it all. It was easy to get sick of the pretentious drinks and the uniform choice of music. But there among the mass of millennials were the friends that I loved with all my heart.

During my many months of depression, my best friend Tom was the one I was always able to talk to; he was the person that I never drew away from. Tom and I fitted together in the way best friends do—we liked the same things and we hated the same people. He studied classics, I was a writer, we talked about books and TV and music. We frantically dissected our lives through the lens of everything from Austen to *The OC*. In recent months, when my retorts turned to wordlessness, he understood. He was happy to sit by my side in silence, he never commented on the slices that I had made up and down my arms.

Tom's girlfriend of ten years, Jessica, was one of our mutual friends from high school. There had always been a push and pull between the two of us—she didn't like how much time I spent with her boyfriend, I didn't like having a curfew placed on my friendship, simply because I was a girl. But Jessica had nothing to worry about—Tom and I weren't friends because we were attracted to each other, we were friends because we understood each other and that was precious.

A couple of weeks after I moved in to Shan-Yi's apartment, I decided to see what it would feel like to leave it for a social event. My friends were headed to the Newington Inn for Karaoke night—I might not be a capable hostess yet, but I figured I would try being part of the crowd. I suppressed the feelings of anxiety and self-doubt—I could do this.

I was always the loud one, the bright one, the bubbly one. Retreating from my friends felt like letting them down. For all of my volume, it was sitting silent on the sidelines that made me feel conspicuous for the first time in my life and began to feel as though I was sitting under a neon sign that read 'damaged' or 'drama'. I wasn't even sure that I knew how to be myself anymore—if I couldn't be bright and bubbly. I wondered if I could be anything at all.

The pub was crowded, but we were one of the biggest groups there. It was difficult to hear over the sound of amateur singers screeching their way through high notes. My friends took turns hitting the stage to the tune of country ballads and old-school Michael Jackson. I could tell from the stern looks being cast across the room that we had upset the equilibrium of karaoke night, dethroning regulars from their long-held slots. But we were having fun.

I picked up a cider at the bar and slid onto a chair next to Tom. He would be my safety net. I wasn't sure what to say as the conversation rattled on around me, friends throwing thoughts and opinions up and down the table. It was hard to get back into the swing of things—I had been absent for so many memories that I couldn't quite keep up.

Everybody knew that I had been having a rough time. My recent life was public gossip, a series of tears at social events, embarrassing incidents that couldn't be washed away. I felt exposed—I wasn't the girl that I was supposed to be.

Still, as the night wore on, I slipped into the gaps of the conversation, finding a voice and putting together words. As a wash of cider swept over me I began to forget the before and after and simply exist in the moment. It was stupid, I knew, to disappear into the mellow of drinking—mixing alcohol with anti-depressants and further confusing my brain. But the cider dislodged my worries and loosened me up at the joints. I didn't care that I was getting drunk, that I didn't know how I'd get home. The evening wasn't as scary as I imagined it to be.

My phone rang while we were at the pub. I wandered out into the carpark until I could hear the voice at the other end. Leaning against my car, I wrapped my arms tight around my chest. I could see my breath on the air. An old friend was calling because she had heard about Shan-Yi's death. It was years since we had spoken on the phone.

'I'm really sorry, Michelle,' she said. 'I know how much Shan-Yi meant to you.'

I was taken aback by the call. I thought that Katherine had forgotten about me—instead she was the first friend to have taken real time to acknowledge Shan-Yi's death. Just hearing her voice say Shan-Yi's name felt strange, as if she was reaching into the depths of me and pulling out something that nobody else had even noticed was there. By the time the phone call ended, I felt winded.

I never realised how many of my close friends didn't know who Shan-Yi was until after she was gone. They didn't understand how she was related to me; didn't know that she was my grandmother. It wasn't the kind of thing that we had done in high school—sat around and discussed our family trees. She was there for all of my milestones, she was introduced to my friends—but somehow, we became dislodged from one another in their minds. We didn't look the same, so we were always separate. We were too confusing.

Still, it felt bizarre and unnatural that they knew so little about her. As though my whole life she had been this secret presence, one that I hadn't even known was a secret.

By the time lights flashed to indicate last drinks, we were all drunk and rowdy—we left the Newington Inn and took to the streets of Petersham en masse. Tom and two of our friends shared a house just a short walk away, so we headed there for beer and warmth and spirits served up straight. As night spilled into early morning we lounged out on the floor and squeezed into the well-worn couches. The residents of the house passed around drinks, each one mixed up stronger than the last. Music played and conversation soldiered on.

When everyone began to disappear home, Tom insisted that I sleep on the couch. I was in no state to drive, and now that I lived on the other side of town I couldn't just wander home like everybody else. With a little persuasion, I curled up on the tiny two-seater, ready to give in to sleep. He tucked me in under a blanket and propped a pillow beneath my head.

As I lay there on the couch he pulled the blanket right up around my shoulders, leaning over my body until his face was so close that our noses grazed. My heart quickened, as though my pulse was directly linked to our proximity. Tom was the person I was closest to in the world, but I still wasn't used to us being *this* close. When he began to speak, his voice was pleading.

'I don't want you to kill yourself.'

It was four in the morning when I woke up. My legs were crammed into the couch, my neck ached, my arms were covered in goose bumps. I was determined to go home. I sat up to put on my shoes and began to creep towards the hallway. As carefully as I stood on my tip toes, the floorboards still creaked under foot. I hadn't even made it out of the living room before I heard footsteps coming towards me. Tom emerged from his bedroom, peering through the darkness.

'Don't go,' he whispered. 'You can't drive.'

'I'll call a taxi,' I said. 'I want to sleep in my own bed.'

'Just stay here.' He stepped into the living room and sat against the arm rest of the couch. As I tried to make my way past him towards the hallway, he pulled me up against him, hands on my waist.

'Stay,' he said again.

'No. I'm going.'

He tugged me closer, one hand running up my neck, the

other down my thigh and right back up again—sliding under my skirt. His fingers gripped my skin, squeezing where they weren't invited. I could smell the beer on his breath.

Frustrated, I pulled away, heading up the hallway towards the front door. My boots thudded against the floor-boards but I didn't care. If anybody woke it would be Tom's fault. I thought about his girlfriend of ten years, Jessica, curled up in his bed.

By the time I got home, I was wide awake. Light began to creep over the south headland, rising up over the Pacific Ocean. With a groan I closed the curtains, creating instant darkness. I ran the night over in my head, re-examining every detail. I was angry that Tom had broken the rules. Our friendship existed by delicate balance, on the grounds of an assurance that it would never become anything else. Even in the dark of the bedroom, I could see the consequences of his actions clear before me. Friendships falling apart—strong friendships, the ones that had survived my depression. I couldn't afford to lose another friend; I couldn't afford to lose Tom. My eyes scanned the rows of books that lined Shan-Yi's bookshelves, stalwart and steady, guarding me from the world.

I should never have left the apartment.

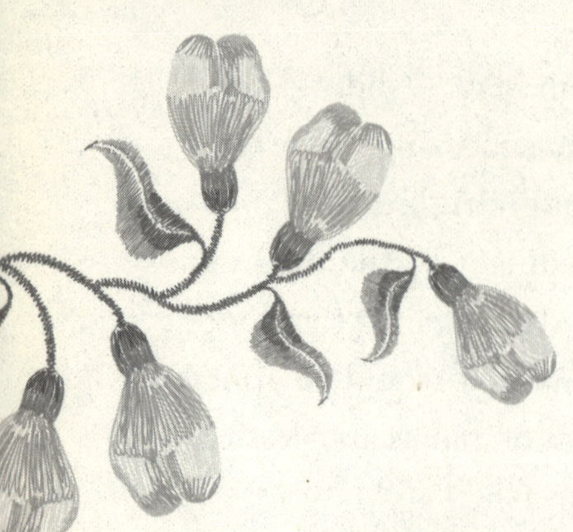

Credits and Deficits

Whenever the girls at Moscow High were brought together, the school hall seemed to explode with chatter. It irritated Alice, the squeals and hubbub, the time it took for the principal to quieten everyone down. At the beginning of 1932, the dean of women from the University of Idaho came to speak to all the female high-school students. Alice was poised with pencil in hand, ready to cover the speech for *The Wocsomian*. Miss Permeal French strode across the stage, her hair pulled into an elegant twist. As she began to speak, Alice took detailed notes, scribbling in shorthand.

'Your high-school days are the formative period in your lives,' said Miss French, her voice ringing across the hall. 'These are the days in which you are beginning to think, to live, to have aspirations and to make friends. These are the days in which you enable those around you to make conclusions about you!'

Alice glanced from side to side, wondering what conclusions her peers might have made about her. She suspected that they didn't really think about her at all. Still, she felt like she was under a microscope.

Miss French set the girls an exercise to complete that evening: compile a list, tallying up the credits and deficits of their character. Obedience, truthfulness, consideration, and courtesy all belonged on the credit side. Parental obedience was the most important of all, since their parents were the most qualified people to judge the girls' characters.

'Your character is choked if you cannot tell the truth,' Miss French continued. 'Be considerate and courteous towards the most forlorn in your community, rather than the most popular.'

This point, at least, was a relief to Alice. Nobody could accuse her of being too popular. Nevertheless, she couldn't help but feel that her character wasn't up to scratch, that her manners and behaviour wouldn't quite meet the dean's standards. She wondered what Miss French would think of her plans to pursue the violin, to travel the world and become a famous musician. She certainly wasn't going to study at the University of Idaho. She hadn't told anybody yet—not even her parents—but Professor Claus had helped her to submit an application to the exclusive performing arts conservatory The Juilliard School of Music in New York. Alice didn't think there'd be too much time for self-reflection and generosity in between rehearsing and exploring her new home.

'Only the worthwhile things count,' Miss French concluded. 'Only our virtues remain with us.'

When the acceptance letter arrived from Juilliard, Alice clutched it to her chest and slept with it under her pillow. The conservatory was so prestigious, so far away that it hardly seemed real—and yet here was a letter with her name on it, inviting her to join its ranks. It took days for her disbelief to give way to excitement. It was really happening, she was off and away. Everything was as she dreamed it would be.

Opportunity

A couple of months after I moved into Shan-Yi's apartment, a job ad appeared in my inbox. A fashion, beauty, and lifestyle website called Flair.com.au was looking for interns. Successful applicants would be contributing articles, sourcing and uploading image galleries, and getting 'right among the action'. They'd need to be available full time during the first week of April for Fashion Week, a requirement that made the role particularly alluring.

I needed a new life—a new course—and here was one just waiting to be taken. The internship wasn't a paid position, but I had the privilege of not paying rent for a little while. I had enough money saved to get by for a few months—if there was ever a time to work for free, this was it. I would only be needed two days a week for the most part—there'd be room for part-time work, and for other projects too. I'd already enrolled in a part-time graphic-design course in the hope it could lead to work—between the course and the internship I could be on my path to an actual career.

I sent my résumé—the new one, polished up by the careers service—off to Flair. I drafted a cover letter bursting with enthusiasm, labouring over every word. The more I thought about the internship, the more I realised I wanted it. It wasn't the path I set out on, it wasn't the dream that I'd had in mind—but as far as fallback plans went, this was a glamorous one. I imagined myself sitting at fashion week, scribbling in a notebook, documenting the latest designs. It seemed like a made-up job, like something from a movie, something beyond the everyday. I could see myself disappearing into that world—I wanted to walk in those shoes.

Fashion was the guilty pleasure that I never really felt guilty about. I believed in fashion—I bought into the hype. Looking around, I saw the entire world speaking in colour and design. Suits and ties as a sign of respect, jeans as freedom, glitter and leather and torn holes as rebellion. As a child I spent hours drawing dresses in the back of my school books, entire collections designed in Crayola and coloured pencil. I was always in a dress, always called a priss—but my clothing made me who I was. If I could combine that feeling with writing, maybe I would be all right.

In Shan-Yi's dressing room, I opened all the wardrobe doors to expose rows of hanging dresses. Half mine, half hers. I was surrounded on three sides by velvet and taffeta, chiffon and satin. We were both over-dressers, there was enough evening wear between the two of us to cater for at least six women.

Each item was squeezed in with precision. Shan-Yi would drape a skirt, top, and jacket over the same hanger—a ready-styled outfit with the appropriate necklace dangling round the hanger's hook. Dresses were hung along with a matching wrap or belt, stockings and bras were still in their packets, half a dozen of the same camisole, presumably her favourite. Shan-Yi *thought* about clothing, her appearance was strategic. It felt right to be pursuing an internship at a fashion website from the glamour of her home. With her taste, determination, and refusal to equivocate, she would probably be better at the job than I would.

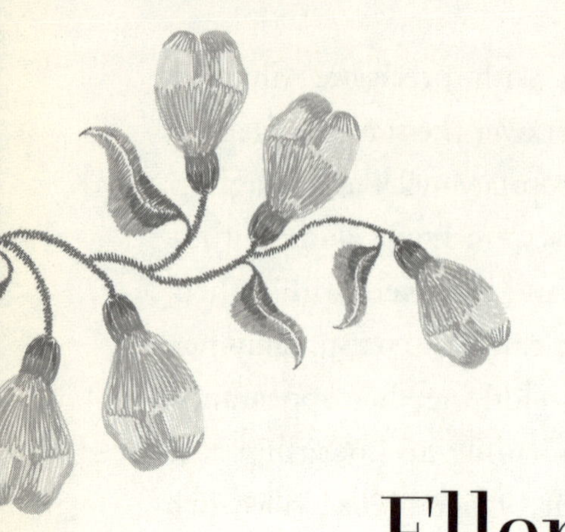

Ellensburg

Yee decided to leave Moscow as quickly as he chose to settle there. In the summer of 1932, there was a chance to invest in a restaurant in the Washington town of Ellensburg—Marie and Mi would take over The Grill and the rest of the Lees would relocate to central Washington. Everything was settled.

Alice's image of life at Juilliard was clear; it was as though she was already there. A life of music in the bustling streets of Manhattan, of orchestras and operas and people just like her. It never occurred to her that her father might not see it so clearly—that it was only in her imagination that the path was set. When Yee told Alice he had enrolled her at the college in Ellensburg it took her a moment to understand what was happening. Her parents began to pack up the house before she could muster up a defence.

'You're not going to New York by yourself,' said Yee.

'You're sixteen years old; you belong with your family.'

She wept as her mother piled her things into boxes, clenched her hands into defiant fists as she watched her books and clothing hauled from her room.

At the centre of Washington state, Ellensburg was the town that everybody passed through—a hub of state highway intersections, the perfect place for tourists and truckers to stop over for the night. What Alice couldn't understand was why anyone would want to stay there. She couldn't see the beauty in the dignified red-brick buildings, didn't stop to enjoy the breeze rolling through the Kittitas Valley grass. She couldn't care less about the rodeo, the jewel of the Ellensburg social calendar. The promise of parades and county fairs, of calf roping and trick riding, provided no compensation for the one thing that Ellensburg lacked entirely—a violin teacher like Carl Claus.

The Lees arrived in June, and Alice was enrolled in summer school at the college. She would start university proper in the fall. The days were long and hot, divided between study and work at the new restaurant. She had always been a good student—graduating from Moscow High eleventh in her class of nearly a hundred—but her grades drooped as her mind drifted up and away from Ellensburg. If it wasn't for her father's constant presence, she mightn't have bothered studying at all.

Alice wasn't the only student at summer school who wished to be someplace else. At lunch she stretched out in the shade with a handful of other students, daydreaming in unison about where they'd rather be. Sometimes they walked into town to eat lunch at the Blue Bird Café, or stopped at the Colonial Theatre after class to see a film. They filled their days with diversions to dull the ache of waiting. Waiting in the summer's haze for life to truly begin.

Alice's friends shared in her misery and anger. They couldn't believe the opportunities that she had already missed. Together, they strategised, plotting her future—as though they would all be living it together. If Alice could make it all the way to New York, then perhaps they all could. If she could make it to Europe, then the world would be at their feet.

An older student, Bernadette Monroe, was her closest confidante. Alice told the eighteen-year-old about Warsing Foo, the wealthy man who had once told her that she belonged in France. She showed Bernadette the letters from Warsing that she kept hidden in her violin case. Bernadette leafed through the sheets of paper as though they were an enthralling novel, she had never read anything like them.

Warsing was Alice's lifeline; he would be her mainstay if she ever left home. As days passed, she found herself thinking of him more and more often. She had his address, she knew she could get in touch. While she sat watching life pass her by in Washington, he was out there in the great wide world—waiting to make all her dreams come true.

Alice had just finished her afternoon walk home from summer school when she found her mother waiting on the front porch—arms crossed, brow knitted.

'Come inside now,' snapped Poon Wong.

As Alice made her way through the narrow hall, she wracked her brain, trying to think what she might have done wrong. She saw Cora, Sammy and Bob huddled in the kitchen—peering through the doorway. Bowing her head, she followed her mother into the living room.

'Mrs Ferguson came into the restaurant,' Poon Wong began, as though this were an indictment in itself. 'She told your father you've been all over town with a boy. She saw you together at the Blue Bird Café, she saw his arm around your shoulders. Why didn't you tell us about this? What are you trying to hide?'

Alice blinked up at her mother's face in silence. She *had* been at the Blue Bird with a boy—Michael, a classmate from summer school. But it hadn't been a secret, she always told her parents when she lunched with friends. Alice was startled by her mother's tone, shocked that she was being asked to defend an innocent friendship. She didn't even know Mrs Ferguson—who was this busybody who watched her every move?

'I was with my friends,' she said. 'I haven't done anything wrong.'

'You haven't done anything wrong?' Poon Wong's usually placid tone was gone. She shook her head in disbelief.

Alice knew that the worst was yet to come. If Poon Wong was this angry, Yee would be even angrier; she couldn't muster up a rage this fierce without her husband's help. Alice wondered what time her father would be home, perhaps she could put herself to bed before the restaurant closed. Her mother approached her and grabbed her by the shoulders.

'When your father comes home he's going to take you to the doctor!'

These last words shocked Alice the most: a scandalous accusation she didn't fully understand. She had no idea what the doctor would do, and no real idea what her parents believed she was guilty of. She stormed to her room, slamming the door behind her. The decision was made before she knew what was happening. She gathered her violin, her coat and her handbag, walked down the stairs and out the front door.

Alice paced the streets of Ellensburg, her mind spinning. Half an hour passed before she managed to gather herself—before she registered where she was and exactly what she was doing. Travelling by muscle memory, she walked towards the college—turning where she always did, following the familiar route. As her thoughts began to settle, her steps took on new purpose. The maple trees waved in the afternoon breeze; she was headed in the right direction.

Yee had already paid for his daughter's summer school tuition but since Alice wasn't going to go to college anymore, she wanted that money back—twelve dollars was just what she needed to escape Ellensburg for good. By the time she met Bernadette out the front of Barge Hall, she was wild with energy, fuelled by fiery indignation. She asked her friend for help and together the pair devised a plan. Bernadette, as the older, more convincing conspirator, would go into the registrar's office and request a refund on behalf of the Lee family. They rehearsed the interaction several times before Bernadette entered the building. Alice spun in circles on the grass, waiting for her friend to re-emerge.

When Bernadette appeared with twelve dollars in hand, Alice felt as though her insides might burst. She could feel her pulse in her fingertips and was startled by their success. In all her life she had never been paid an allowance—her handbag was empty but for a handkerchief, a comb, and a key to the house—and this was more than she'd ever seen. She folded the notes and tucked them into her handbag. She supposed she should feel guilty, but as far as she could see it, these twelve dollars were Yee's investment in her future and that was exactly how she would spend them—on reaching her greatest potential.

Clasping her handbag tight against her chest, she thanked her friend twice over. When they said their farewells she wondered when she would see Bernadette again, if ever. But there was no time to fear or fret, her exit door was swinging wide open—who knew when it might slam shut? She kissed Bernadette goodbye and headed straight on through it.

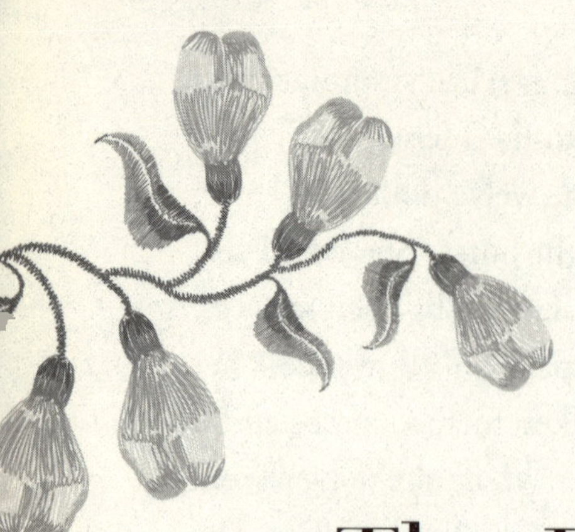

The Interview

The Flair office was like a Kardashian's fever dream: hot-pink pillows arranged on ornate black armchairs, the Flair logo encrusted on them in diamantes; a mirror-glass coffee table on a leopard-print rug; Parisian scenes on the walls, fresh flowers in vases. It was an open, collaborative workspace full of natural light that bounced off polished floorboards. It was garish and kitsch but I liked it—this wasn't just an office; this room was somebody's passion.

Holly, the online producer at Flair, had emailed through a series of exercises for me to complete in advance of the interview—articles to write in order to demonstrate my skills and galleries of the latest runway trends to compile. I had spread out on the living-room floor with books and magazines scattered around me, leafing through glossy pages and taking notes, connecting ideas with arrows and exclamation points, before sending my work back to Flair. I spent days preparing for the interview and my head was full of memorised answers to hypothetical questions.

I wore an outfit selected after hours of trial and error. Sitting down on an armchair I crossed one leg over the other, placing my hands on my lap, conscious of my every move. Holly was younger than I expected—she looked to be in her mid-twenties like me and we slipped into easy conversation. She told me about Flair, about their vision for a luxury publication that cut through the clutter of the internet with high quality, expert lifestyle advice. She spoke of the celebrities they collaborated with and the various experts who contributed pieces to the site. I liked the sound of the work they were doing, was impressed with their commitment to quality content. With such a professional approach and such high-calibre contributors, I was surprised I had never heard of the site before. When she told me that the team liked the pieces I sent through, my shoulders relaxed a little—my broad smile felt less forced.

Maja, the founder and editor-in-chief, strode into the office halfway through the interview and introduced herself with a firm handshake, her nails perfectly manicured, a gold bracelet jingling as we shook. Leaning against a desk, she repeated Holly's words with heightened intensity. I was struck by her passion and her no-nonsense demeanour. These were intelligent, ambitious women, proud of the work they were doing.

When I returned to Shan-Yi's apartment, I paced around, reliving the interview over and over again. I cringed at the thought of some of my answers, second guessed myself and wondered how I'd done. But as I moved through the space, the rooms looked somehow different than they had before. I saw new possibilities where before there was dust and clutter. The panels of polished wood and gilded door handles glinted in the afternoon light. Could this apartment be the backdrop to a career in digital publishing?

The Detour

Alice headed for Seattle. It was a detour, of course, but twelve dollars wouldn't get her to New York—and besides, her position at Juilliard had already been declined. To make it all the way to France, she would need Warsing's help, so she settled instead on the closest big city that she knew of. Once the five-dollar bus fee was paid for, she would have money left over for food and lodging. By the time the sun began to set she was already on her way.

She stared across the landscape as the bus trundled through vast plains, spotted by small towns. She thought about Miss Permeal French, the dean who valued 'parental obedience' above all and shuddered to imagine what the woman would think of her running away from home. Alice's tally of character traits was tipping over to the deficit side—selfishness, impulsiveness, disobedience. But the path she had chosen was the only one that remained before her. She had to pursue the violin, had to focus on music. It was what she was—the one thing that made her special. If she stayed in Ellensburg she might never be anything at all.

Darkness fell as the bus climbed into the mountains. It was as though the bus and the sun were rising and falling in counter balance, one driving the other. The forest of heaven-high pines blotted out any moonlight—she could see nothing out the window but her own reflection. How had she come to be on this bus, surrounded by strangers, on her way to an unfamiliar city?

When Alice stepped off the bus in Seattle, the city continued to scurry about its business, but somehow, it felt as if the whole world was watching. She was used to walking down the streets of Moscow by herself, but those excursions had never felt like this. This was the first time she had ever been *truly* alone. The space between Alice and the strangers around her seemed to expand as she hurried forwards, head down. It was like the space between a musician and her audience, a space that placed her on show. Everything was loud and bright, the world was more vivid than ever before.

There was no time to explore the city—she needed to find somewhere to stay and she needed to contact Warsing. At a coffee shop near the auto stand she asked after nearby boarding houses. She beat her toe against the floor while a waitress scrawled an address onto a napkin. The scent of greasy fries and floor wax hung in the air. As she wandered back into the evening she noticed a man sitting at the counter, watching her

Alice Lee, age four, near Spokane, Washington, in the summer of 1921.

Yee, Poon Wong, Marie, Alice and Cora Lee in Spokane 1925.

Alice Lee (front left), fourteen, with the girls of the sophomore class at Moscow High, 1931.

One of many portraits taken of Alys Maier in her early twenties.

Mi Lew and Marie Lee Lew on their wedding day in Moscow, Idaho, 1932.

Shan-Yi Balogh photographed by William G Buckle in Sydney.

Alice Lee (second from left), playing violin with the University of Idaho Symphony Orchestra while still a high school sophomore in 1931.

Alys Maier, 21, photographed with her violin in Bombay, November 1937.

Portrait of Andrew 'Bandi' Balogh, 31, in 1937.

Alys Maier (seated in star headband) at a dress up night on-board the SS Julio Cesare during her years of travel with Karl, September 1937.

Alys Maier visits the Taj Mahal during her travels with Karl, 1937.

Alys Maier meets her father in law in Rome, October 1937.

Portrait of Karl Maier, 32, 1940.

Alys Maier, age twenty-two, on board the SS Oronsay, 1938.

Alys Maier, photographed by Karl Maier, in their apartment on Macleay Street in Elizabeth Bay, Sydney, 1939.

Alys Maier, and best friend Margot Adams (later Margot Martyn) together in 1940.

Andrew Balogh, age thirty-nine, and son Albin Balogh, eleven, on the day of Andrew's Australian naturalisation, 11 May 1945.

Shan-Yi Balogh and Andrew Balogh, walking in Sydney's central business district, circa 1950.

over the top of his coffee cup. She clutched the napkin tightly.

The city looked like a scene from one of the Hollywood films that she watched at the Kenworthy Theatre in Moscow. Seattle was but a miniature of New York—still she couldn't imagine a larger city, a more complete picture of everything she'd envisioned New York to be. Making her way to the boarding house, she blinked up at the inferno of lights—flickering neon signs and glowing streetlamps, glinting off the steel backs of electric trams. Through the windows of diners, she watched couples bent close, deep in a world of their own. All around her the crowds wove rhythmically along the sidewalk, like members of a big band, stepping to the beat. She saw a woman walking with her arms full of flowers, peonies dripping from the bouquet as her date lent close. A group of wild boys with suspenders and cigarettes hurried past; one tipping his hat to her.

The boarding house was above a tobacconist and the stairs creaked underfoot as she climbed to the second floor. Alice held her breath, putting on a poised face. As she emerged from the stairwell she saw a circle of women sitting around a table playing cards. Their faces were old and young, ugly and beautiful, but their eyes were all knives—they pierced straight into her. Wind blew through the room; the women were rugged up in coats. There were runs in their stockings, multi-storey ladders and holes big enough to slide a fist through. Alice thought of her mother's disappointment any time she or Cora came home from school with a run in their stockings.

'Can I help you?' one of the women said, rising from her seat.

'No, thank you,' said Alice. 'I've come to the wrong place.'

She fled back down the stairs. If she stayed in the boarding house she wouldn't last more than a couple of nights. She'd be back home with her tail between her legs, begging her father's forgiveness.

A doorman welcomed her into the lobby of the Bergonian Hotel, bowing his head as he held the door open. Plush armchairs stood on Persian rugs, lamps cast a warm glow. Alice strode across the room and approached the reception desk, her head held high. She knew that the money left in her purse wouldn't be enough to pay for a room, but she hoped that with confidence and enough poise she could talk her way into the hotel.

'I need a room,' she said. She tipped her nose upwards, trying to give the air of an aristocrat. 'My luggage and money are on their way, but I'll need a room in the meantime.'

The concierge raised his brow. His eyes darted over her, scepticism written across his face. She sought out his gaze and held it steady with her own, mustering up her best impatient stare.

'Of course, Ma'am.'

'Thank you,' she said, as though she didn't care. 'And I'll need to send a telegram.'

By the time she got to her room, it felt like days had passed since she'd left Ellensburg. She thought of her mother standing on the porch, her siblings huddled in the kitchen. She fell heavy onto the bed, sinking into its depths without bothering to remove her clothes. She was safe and she was warm, she had a bed to sleep in and a door to lock behind her. As for what would come next, that could wait until the morning.

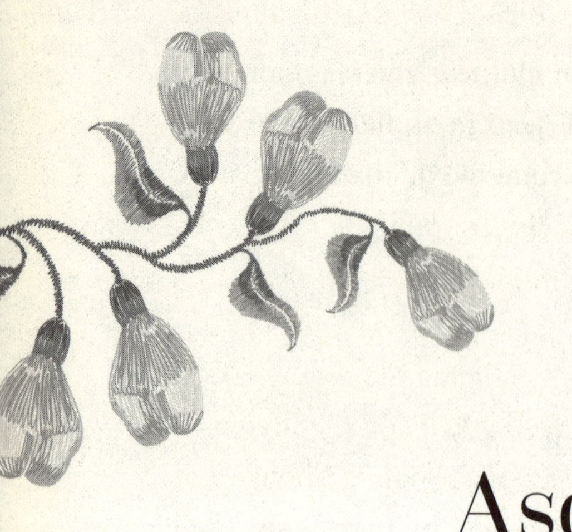

Ascent

Summer in Bellevue Hill smells like jasmine and sea salt. I breathed in deep as I stood on Shan-Yi's balcony, my thoughts tumbling out over the hills and harbour below. My bare feet pressed against the tiles where hers had been. There was so much possibility in the view which belonged to both of us.

The days were hot, as though my excitement about the internship radiated through the whole city. Every afternoon I ran down the steep slope to Rose Bay, then all the way back up again. I had never been a runner before, but the lush streets and boat-speckled harbour drew me out into the air. It's a strange neighbourhood, beautiful but quiet.

Where I grew up, in Summer Hill, there are always people out on the street—teenagers mucking about on bicycles or skateboards, parents walking kids to and from school. It's a suburb of dense terraces and semi-detached Victorian houses, of front doors pushing right up against the footpath. People drink cups of tea on their front verandahs and hang about chatting at flimsy open gates, their conversations interrupted by the comforting soundtrack of aircraft noise. The streets are more concrete than grass, but everyone wants to get out and enjoy them.

I didn't personally know all my neighbours on my childhood street, but I knew what they looked like. In Bellevue Hill my neighbours were invisible. Their palatial houses sat at the end of long driveways, concealed by high fences and dense greenery. Cars emerged in the morning and disappeared back behind gates at night. Running down the hill to Rose Bay I felt as if the whole suburb belonged to me. I couldn't decide if it was eerie or wonderful.

I began to love the searing pain that came with catapulting forward—the lingering aches and the deep sleep that followed. The loop I ran wasn't long—just under three kilometres—but the ascent up Cranbrook Road felt as though my chest might split open. It was the kind of agony that was fierce enough to distract me from my inner monologue. At first, I could only make it about ten metres up the hill, then it was a little further, and a little further after that. I was improving, a metre at a time, marking my progress by memorising gateposts and flowerbeds.

At night, I stretched out exhausted in front of the TV, which in practice meant lying in bed with my laptop. When I had the energy, I would poke around the cupboards, sifting through old clothes and records. Sorting out Shan-Yi's belongings and packing them into boxes was a condition of my residency. I tried on her clothes, designing outfits to wear on my first week of work. The majority of the dresses were far too small, but there were a handful that fit, and others that were even too big. Her shoes were tiny, too narrow for me to even fit my toes in. It was a wardrobe composed over the course of her life—a tailored map of Shan-Yi.

The more I uncovered, the less I felt that I knew her. Every cabinet that I opened exposed a bevy of new questions. Where had she worn the kimonos? Why had she been studying German? In what country was this or that photograph taken? The smaller questions raised bigger ones—great expanses of her life that I knew nothing about. I did know that she loved chicken wings, Peking duck, and chocolate cake; that she insisted on taking the leftovers home from a restaurant. She called it a 'puppy bag' instead of a 'doggy bag' because she thought it was cuter. I knew that she hated being told what to do. When she first bought a microwave, the user's manual said not to use the appliance for cooking eggs. The first thing she did was put an egg in, determined to see what would happen. The resulting explosion took hours to clean up. I knew that she played a lot of tennis, and that it wasn't until her mid-seventies that she replaced the sport with bridge. Above the bar were dozens of trophies, golden women swinging rackets, and miniature hands holding fanned cards. I knew that she had her hair set once a week, that she hated technology and always wore black and gold clothing with big jade jewellery. And I knew she liked tacky knick-knacks—little plastic robots that whirred across a table, rubber finger puppets in the shape of growling monsters. When she bought them for us as children, she always bought one for herself. I knew the sound of her voice—her mixed accent—and the feel of her crumpled skin.

But these were small things, fragments that centred around the final twenty years of her life. As close as I thought we were, the seventy years that came before were a mystery.

Seattle

Days passed and no word came from Warsing. The handful of coins in Alice's purse began to shrink. She slept in her blouse, shaking it out when she woke to smooth the wrinkles. Rising early, she spent her mornings walking along the edge of the Sound, where the scent of salt and pines mingled in the air. For breakfast she ate an apple from the market at Pike Place, for lunch she ate bread—but even these small meals were getting too expensive.

She wondered what would happen if she never heard from Warsing. Back in Ellensburg she was preoccupied by his doting letters, by his tailored suits and fine leather shoes, the hotels and restaurants he visited abroad. She remembered his affection and his wealth—she was too focused on these splendid details to consider the fact that she might not be able to reach him at all. She had been so certain that he would help her, so certain he would be waiting for her. The idea that he might *not* be was terrifying. How would she pay the hotel if he didn't send money? How would she support herself? But she pushed the fear aside; it was too late to be frightened now, too late to go home.

At night, she curled up by the fire in the ladies' lounge, scanning the newspaper for a job. By day, she visited nearby boutiques and department stores.

'You're lovely,' said the manager at the luxurious Nordstrom's department store. 'We'll dress you in a kimono and put you in the oriental section. Come back in December.'

Alice would be dead of starvation by December.

One evening Alice came across an ad in the paper—two artists, a couple, were looking for a model. She caught a tram across town to the international district to meet them. In the couple's apartment, there were paintings all over the walls, dirty plates and half-eaten meals piled up on the mantelpiece. As Alice moved into the living room, the woman scooped up the plates and filled a cup with coffee, the stained rings on the glass pot disappeared under the brew.

'Would you like a cup?'

Alice liked them immediately. They were friendly and asked questions about why she had come to the city and how often she would be available to pose. When she told them about her music they were fascinated and asked her to bring her violin the next time. She sculled her coffee and wolfed down a plate of crackers. The woman's eyes followed her every move.

'Would you like an advance?'

'Yes, please!' said Alice. '… if you don't mind.'

'This should keep you going until Monday.' The woman pushed two dollars into Alice's hand, closing her fingers over the notes. 'We'll see you at ten.'

The neighbourhood was full of Chinese restaurants and stores. Right around the corner Alice passed a candied fruit store, selling the kind of sweets she'd eaten as a child. The window was full of dried fruits in colourful wrappers, preserved lemon and ginger, candied plums and salted lotus seeds. She could see all of her favourite candies—the kind her father bought for Christmas in Spokane.

She walked into the store and selected a lavish box of candies, as many as two dollars would buy. When she emerged she had no money left to pay for her tram fare back to the Bergonian, but she didn't care. She walked the one and a half miles, eating all the way. The shrivelled plums were sweet and sour, just as she remembered them. The salty flavour left her wanting more. She munched on sugary disks of pressed hawthorn fruit, throwing the wafers down as though they were potato chips. Spiced nuts cut through the sweetness, but by the time she arrived back at the hotel she felt nauseous. The box was empty; her money gone.

Day and night Alice walked the Seattle streets, crossing back and forth until she knew the city by heart. Pike, Pine, Union, University, she memorised street names, mapped out intersections in her mind. She couldn't afford to go to the theatre or to the pictures, but she liked to walk past ticket booths and watch the swarming crowds. Her eyes followed women in their sweeping satin gowns, men in top hats, their pocket handkerchiefs folded in neat peaks. These revellers strolled without glancing left or right, their lives so lavish that they didn't need to take notice of anybody else. Alice imagined herself fitting in there—pointing her nose upwards and ignoring the rest of the crowd. When she grew tired of people watching she roamed the department stores, where everything was clean and bright.

She had been in the city for over a week. She washed her clothes in the hotel bathroom, but she knew that she was beginning to look scruffy. She scrubbed her face with soap and combed her heavy hair—hoarded complimentary toiletries, the only possessions she had. However far she'd come, she was still Poon Wong's daughter; she wanted to present herself with care. But the hotel staff were asking about her luggage, reminding her of her unsettled bill. She brushed aside their queries with a wave of the hand.

'As I said, my things are coming. My money is coming,' she replied, feigning a confidence she no longer felt.

She was wandering down Third Avenue one evening when a stranger asked her to go dancing. She rushed to say yes, any company was better than none at all. The man could have been as old as her father, but she trusted the smile caught in his grizzled blond beard. He laughed like a honking goose. Together, they went to an underground nightclub where patrons pressed up against one another, swinging to the hullabaloo of a rollicking jazz band. She didn't know how to dance but he held her tight, she hung from his shoulders while they swayed through the room. She took sips of dark brown liquor that burned her throat and left her dizzy.

Later he took her to a diner, where they had coffee and lemon pound cake. She talked about her life back in Moscow and Ellensburg. She had just begun to tell him stories from high school when he excused himself to go to the bathroom. By the time she finished her slice of cake he still hadn't returned. She waited at the table, watching strangers out the window while her fellow diners slowly filtered out. A waiter approached her and bent down close.

'Your friend settled the bill,' he whispered. 'I don't think he's coming back.'

As she walked back to the hotel, the streets were dark and empty. A taxi cab cruised slowly by, scanning the sidewalks for a passenger. In the early morning quiet, she wondered what she'd done wrong.

At peak hours, when the hotel was buzzing, Alice liked to look down over the lobby from the safety of the mezzanine. She felt safe in the ladies' lounge; the women had comforting faces and easy smiles, they were the wives and daughters of businessmen, they jiggled babies in their arms. She leant against the gilded railing, watching as the guests sat in armchairs, as porters carried bags back and forth. Parents hurried their children in and out, carrying jackets and bags, holding tiny hands. It was comforting to imagine their lives, to make up their stories, to give them names. The trick was to live in the moment, to put one foot in front of the other and just keep going.

There were writing desks in the lobby and one night she stood and watched a man scribble away below. She recognised him, she had seen him around the hotel before. His work ethic was transfixing—he sat there for hours, filling page after page. Looking down at him from above she wondered what he was writing, wondered what was keeping him occupied.

'Writing home?' the question escaped her before she knew it was coming, her voice falling down from the mezzanine to the man below. It was days since she had spoken to a soul.

The young man turned his head to see her, blinking for a moment and then dropping his pen. He raced up the staircase to the mezzanine, where Alice had dropped into an armchair, startled by his approach. He drew a second armchair up to hers and took a seat beside her.

'You are the most beautiful woman I have ever seen.'

Donald didn't believe Alice's story about staying penniless at the Bergonian, awaiting word from a man in China who would take her away to France—but he liked the blunt candour with which she spoke. She claimed to be sixteen but by the looks of her she was more like twenty-three. Still, there was a sincerity and innocence that cut through her madness, some truth to her story of being lost and alone. She might be a wild adventuress, but he felt compelled to take her under his wing. He wanted to see where her tale would go.

Despite her initial surprise, Alice soon relaxed into Donald's kindness. He seemed interested in her story and she was glad to have somebody to talk to. He was young, single, and lived full-time at the hotel. Alice had never heard of somebody *living* in a hotel. Life at the Bergonian was easiest, he said, for a bachelor. A newspaper man, he was the art editor of the *Seattle Post Intelligencer.* She told him about her work on *The Wocsomian*, all the articles she had written about life at Moscow High. He could already tell she was full of wonderful stories and he was keen to hear them all.

Intern

Entering the conversation at Flair was like stepping into the middle of a grand slam tennis match. Maja, Holly, and Anna effortlessly slung inside jokes and industry gossip back and forth across the room and I kept up as best I could, seduced by their whiplash dialogue. It was just the three of them in the office—the founder and editor-in-chief, the online producer, and the beauty editor. Everybody else who contributed to Flair was a guest expert, a freelancer or, in my case, an intern. But the scarcity of full-time staff wasn't reflected in the final product—Flair was a full-bodied publication, rougher around the edges than the websites of *Marie Clare* or *Vogue*, but producing content at a pace that suggested a much larger team. Ads for Burberry, Chanel and Estée Lauder streamed down the sides of the page—serious players were taking a bet on Flair.

Maja was the quintessential lifestyle entrepreneur, flying from one place to the next, carrying a laptop, sculling a coffee, donning the studded Valentino heels that everybody was coveting. She wore Diane von Furstenberg wrap dresses and had her hair blown out once a week, always in the same bouncy style. She knew what she liked and what she disliked, and saw little grey in between. With the air of someone who had been everywhere and seen everything, she'd figured out exactly who she was. Whether it was knowing what to wear for her figure, what colour worked for her hair, what movies were good and what music was terrible, there was no need to experiment anymore. She hated young indie starlets who were crass and broke the established rules, who made pop culture references that she didn't understand. She loved Karl Lagerfeld and Sofia Loren; icons who were eternal. She loved being in the office, around her team—the centre of attention and running the show. Her background wasn't in writing or editing, but business—she'd started Flair as an online store, shifting into publishing during the financial crisis. Her motto was: 'Never blame yourself. Own it, forgive yourself, and then move on'.

Ducking in and out, she suggested ideas, critiqued articles, and then disappeared again to a meeting or a lunch. Somehow she balanced motherhood too, negotiating the limits of time in a way that made it all appear effortless. The rest of us worked fast—writing pieces, pulling together image galleries, replying to emails from PR agents, advertisers, and contributors. The soundtrack to our work was the dinging of the doorbell as courier after courier arrived with deliveries. The bread and butter of Flair was beauty, and every new product arrived with the hope of being featured on the site. Nail polish and contour kits, hairspray and lipstick—mounds of unopened packages piled up on desks.

When I applied for the job, I fantasised about attending events, drinking champagne, and writing about the runway. But I never expected the reality to live up to the fantasy. As much as I daydreamed about becoming the next Anna Wintour or Grace Coddington, I mostly expected to make photocopies and run errands. The biggest shock of interning at Flair was how much it really did live up to the fantasy. Life at Flair was glamorous and I was actually contributing to the site. Where the job differed from my fantasies was that there were no photoshoots or layout books, no days to spend massaging articles to perfection. Flair was a digital publication, so there was nothing to be photocopied—no paper in sight—and there was no time to be wasted. Sparkling new content had to be generated every day—to make that happen, it was essential that everyone be on their game.

Just a few weeks into my internship, I was sent to events. There was a constant schedule of product launches that couldn't be missed. Maja preferred to send staff in her place and Holly and Anna were tied up with the responsibilities of keeping the website live and running, so events largely fell to the interns—making an unpaid gig at Flair more exciting than most.

I drank cocktails at The Ivy while listening to a sales pitch on skincare products, ate breakfast at Café Sydney while learning about jojoba oil. For the launch of a crème blush, I attended a crème brulée making class at an elegant French restaurant; for the rebranding of an Italian hair conditioner I learnt to make pasta from scratch. PR agencies were always trying to devise some new way to make their event stand out from the last—to make the moisturiser that they were spruiking seem different from every other moisturiser on the market. The result was a constant flood of invitations to this or that hot new venue, to sample some fabulous new thing. For the pack of beauty editors who made their way from place to place, day after day, the lustre of launches wore thin. But to an intern, eating free food and drinking free booze at several events a week, the beauty world was paradise.

Lying in bed each night marvelling at the flashy escapades of the day, it was hard to imagine that there'd ever been a time when I thought I had nothing to live for.

Miss Lee

Alice and Donald dined together every night. At six o'clock he was hat in hand, waiting for her in the lobby. He watched the staircase until she appeared, always in the same little skirt and coat. Sometimes they went to see a film or a show, other times they lingered over dinner and dessert. They explored the city he knew so well—he played the tour guide, soaking up familiar streets with brand new eyes. Each night, before they left the Bergonian, she took care to tell the concierge where they were going and how she could be reached. Donald asked, 'Don't you trust me?'

'Of course I do, it's just that if my friend calls, I need to make sure he knows where I am – that I haven't left.'

Donald never gave her money, although he kept her very well fed. She always ate as though she'd been fasting all day. She was gorging on pork chops at the Purple Pup Diner one evening when the waitress approached their table.

'Miss Lee?' she said. 'There's a call for you at the Bergonian.'

They left their dinner unfinished and hurried back to the hotel. She bid him a rushed goodnight in the lobby and ran up to her room to take the call. Perched on the bed she wrapped herself up in a blanket, overcome by an onset of shivers.

'Hello? Warsing?'

The line crackled. She could hear voices in the background. 'London calling,' 'Berlin calling.' She held the phone to her ear for half an hour before she finally heard Warsing's voice. He sounded a million miles away and only a few words were able to pass between them on the poor line.

'I'll send you a ticket. We'll meet in Hong Kong.'

The next morning Alice received a telegram from Warsing. She was to visit the First National Bank, just around the corner from the hotel. Stepping out into the brisk Seattle air, she was overcome with relief. She had barely slept but she was full of energy, her mind reeling with thoughts of the future. It was never her plan to return to Hong Kong but the thought of moving forward at all came as a welcome relief. She wasn't going straight to Paris, but at least she was going *somewhere*.

When she arrived at the bank, the manager was waiting to greet her at the door. 'Miss Lee!' he beamed. 'I'm Martin Harrison. Please join me in the office.'

The bank was dark and gloomy. Tellers stood in ornate booths, protected by wrought-iron bars. As Alice and the manager made their way through the room, the tellers turned their heads in unison. She felt as though she was on trial, her footsteps echoing across the marble floor.

'We've received your deposit,' said Mr Harrison, pouring a cup of tea and placing it before her. 'We've drawn up the paperwork to open an account in your name. We look forward to assisting you with anything you might need.'

'I don't need an account,' she said. 'I'd just like the money please.'

The manager's eyebrows shot up. 'Miss Lee, you've received five thousand dollars.'

'Thank you,' she replied. 'May I take cash?'

'Are you *sure*?'

'Yes.'

What use did she have for a bank account in Seattle? She was about to leave for Hong Kong. Who knew when she'd be back.

Mr Harrison stared at the woman before him, unsure of what to say. She was so confident and clear, her tone resolute. He was used to dealing with husbands and fathers—men who understood the inherent risk of carrying large amounts of cash and knew that five thousand dollars was enough to purchase a six-bedroom home.

As Alice squeezed the notes into her handbag, she felt a great weight lift from her shoulders. She was thrilled that Warsing had sent so much, excited to finally have money of her own. The tellers dropped their work and whispered as she walked out the door.

That night, she bought Donald dinner. When she finished telling him everything that had happened, he made her go back to the beginning and start again, leaning in close to make sure he heard her right. She was frustrated by his confusion; they had discussed her plans before. But by the time she finished for the second time, he was looking at her as though it was the very first time they'd met.

The next day Donald hired a car and pulled up in front of the hotel. Alice climbed in and they took off through the streets, wind ruffling her hair. They drove out into the suburbs, through houses perched on steep hills. Soon there were no more houses, just trees and the winding road. They climbed right up to a hilltop that looked out over Seattle.

The wind was so fierce when she got out of the car, she worried it might bowl her over. But Donald hooked his arm in hers, held her steady as they walked down to the lookout.

Alice could see the tops of all the buildings, the steeples of the churches, the pinnacle of Smith Tower. She could see all the way out over Puget Sound, watch the ferries as they crisscrossed the great expanse of blue. Donald pointed out Bainbridge Island, a mass of trees that disappeared into the mountain range beyond.

She thought of her family, out beyond the mountains. It had been three weeks since she had seen them, but it felt like a lifetime. She felt as though they were people she had known in a dream, people who lived in a place that wasn't quite real. Nevertheless, she missed them deep in her bones. She couldn't remember her last visit to Seattle, that day long ago when she, her mother, and Marie had travelled down the channel of water stretched out before her. She tried to imagine Marie as a small child, tried to imagine her own body strapped to her tiny mother's back. But thinking of Marie and her mother made her feel unsteady. She relegated their faces to the corners of her mind and focused on the future—Warsing was waiting for her on the other side of the globe. The path ahead was unsteady, but she trusted him. When she was just twelve years old, he had been determined to make her a star. Now she was sixteen—practically a woman—and her musicianship was more accomplished than ever. He would guide her forward; he would know what to do. His was the only face that mattered now.

She stood there for a long time—rooted in place, looking out over the view. Her hair battered her face, a squirrel scampered across the ground before her. She was excited, she was alive. It felt as though the wind was blowing right through her, the crisp Washington air rushing the blood through her veins. For the first time ever it occurred to her that she might miss this country.

When Donald spoke she was startled, drawn back down from her drifting thoughts. Her mind raced to catch up with his words as he took her hand and asked her to marry him. She gaped up at her friend as he bent down towards her. He looked at her as though he wanted to pin her with his eyes, to hold her in place with the intensity of his gaze. She didn't know what to do, but she believed him when he told her he loved her. She was certain he was speaking from the heart.

For a moment she considered what it would be like to stay in Seattle with Donald. They could start a life together, two bohemians—the art editor and the musician. But the image faded as quickly as it appeared. Alice had given her word to Warsing, she *had* to go to Hong Kong.

Seattle was already a memory, her future was waiting.

A White Evening Dress

If Alice never saw her old clothes again it would be too soon. Her stockings were worn thin, her coat smelled musty and stale. Each time she wrung the soap from her blouse and skirt—scrubbing them in the hotel basin—it was difficult to restrain herself from tossing them out the window. But for weeks they were all that she had. Now, with Warsing's money in hand, she could buy whatever she wanted. There was a bounce in her step as she strode through town.

I. Magnin stood on the corner of Union and Fifth, opulent in its six storeys. She had passed the department store several times on her way to the Fifth Avenue Theatre with Donald. Now, she could count herself among the stylish customers who passed in and out of the immense boutique. With her cash in her purse, she pushed against the great brass door handle and climbed the marble steps. A shop assistant appeared by her side.

'I don't know much about clothes,' said Alice. 'But I need everything. I have absolutely nothing and I can pay in cash.'

The assistant was delighted to show her around, sweeping up dresses and coats for her to try. Having never had money of her own before, the thrill of spending was electric. She bought a suitcase and handbags, daytime clothes and cocktail dresses, shoes, handbags, underwear and negligees—everything she could think of that she might possibly need.

With the help of several staff she picked out a white evening dress. It was a simple gown, sweeping, and made of fine white cloth. She didn't tell the shop assistants what she needed it for, although she wondered if they could guess. In truth, she didn't want to say the words out loud, didn't want to give voice to the fears she kept buried. But the fears infected her voice on their own—her throat tightened, her words were tangled. The formal-wear department felt hotter than the rest of the store.

A few days after her visit to I. Magnin, Alice sent Warsing a telegram.

'Money all gone. Please send more for ticket and pocket money.'

Warsing's reply was immediate.

'Ticket booked on the SS President Cleveland. *Pocket money in Hong Kong.'*

When Alice left the Bergonian, she took care to leave the room exactly as she had found it. She tucked the sheets in tight and smoothed down the pillows, took pride in polishing the bathroom with a towel. Her new clothes and new shoes where packed into new leather suitcases. She left a generous tip for the porter—as if to say 'See! I told you to be patient.' Walking down the hall she let out a great sigh, just as she had on her first night in Seattle. When she thought about her relief—crawling into the hotel bed in her clothes—it felt like a memory from her childhood. Now she need never wear those clothes again.

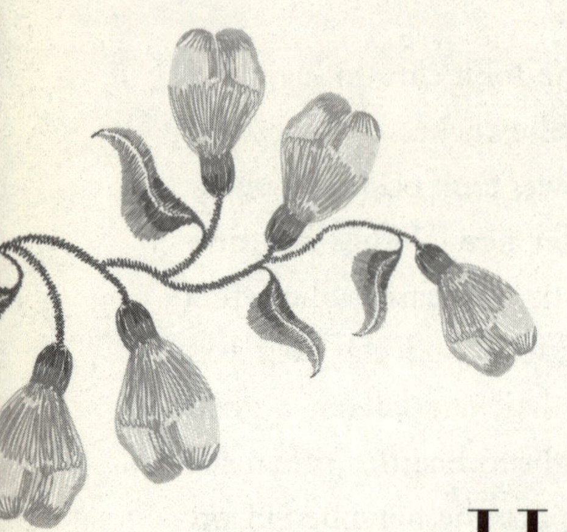

Hostess

I watched myself in Shan-Yi's mirror. Getting dressed, putting on my face, starting and ending the day in her dressing room. I was lit by the rows of golden lightbulbs, framed by her wardrobe doors. My world was all aglow.

I wore a costume to work. Sleek black or white dresses, five-inch heels, burgundy lipstick. I played a character—the bubbly intern, bursting with enthusiasm, ready to get down to work. I laughed and gossiped, walked through the door with a tray of coffees and a smile. At Flair, the last year of my life didn't exist—there was no depression. It wasn't important *how* I managed to score an apartment in Bellevue Hill, the important part was that I had one—even if it wasn't my own.

I watched myself transform in her mirror. I looked better every day—more confident, more in control, more cool. The apartment grew smaller as I grew bigger. I strode across it, filling it with life, until it felt like mine. I no longer had time to poke through cupboards or riffle through knick-knacks.

After years of floundering I had found what I was looking for—a yardstick to mark my success by. You can't be successful without something to be successful *at*, you can't succeed without criteria to check off with a great big tick. I was only an intern—living on packaged soup, canned tuna, and toast—but I was suddenly successful in the most conspicuous of ways. My Instagram feed was a long ribbon of flashy events, free swag, and life around Bellevue Hill. I had achievable goals, my very own set of concrete stepping stones to leap across. The more successful I felt, the less I was afraid.

I began to invite everybody in. I hosted pre-drinks before nights out on Oxford Street in Surry Hills, served lunches out on the balcony. I spent long afternoons with my girlfriends, our feet propped up on the railing, the harbour breeze in our hair. I threw parties—a Halloween party with spider webs hanging from the chandeliers, jack-o-lanterns sitting on the bar. For my twenty-fifth birthday, a *Great Gatsby* party with pearls and flapper dresses, so perfect for the decor it almost felt like the real thing.

From time to time, I went back to my parents' for dinner—and invited them over to the apartment too—but my days and nights grew more social. I struggled to find free time rather than to fill it. I was spending all my savings on chips and booze, on making decorations out of craft paper and glue. But it was worth it for long nights getting lost in the soft light.

My friends were split in their verdict of the apartment.

Half of them thought it was an absolute palace, the remainder thought it looked like the hotel from *The Shining*—they couldn't imagine being able to sleep there without nightmares of Jack Nicholson bursting through doors, brandishing a knife. Tom was the one person who seemed to love the place in the same way that I did. He saw what I saw, a piece of history, a once-in-a-lifetime opportunity to disappear into the past.

It was easy to be angry with Tom when I wasn't around him. For weeks after the karaoke night I was outraged by his behaviour—angry on behalf of his girlfriend, angry because of our friendship. I couldn't shake the feeling that he had taken something from me—a friend I could really count on. Right when I was struggling the most, my intelligent, reliable best friend had devolved into the cliché of a drunk and horny male.

But it was harder to remain angry when we were face to face. The next time we were together, I couldn't help but let go of my anger and slip back into hanging out with my friend. I started to wonder what I had been so upset about—it was hardly a crime to be drunk and stupid. I was probably overreacting, probably just being self-righteous. I let go of my anger, piece by piece, and before long everything looked the same, just in a slightly different colour.

Hong Kong

Shan-Yi learnt to dance on board the *President Cleveland*. With the other first-class passengers, she played quoits and shuffleboard on the sunny deck, put together costumes for fancy-dress evenings. When the ship finally drew into Hong Kong's Victoria Harbour, she was sorry to say goodbye to its breezy luxury. She hugged her new friends tight and blew kisses to the engineer and the chief purser. She could feel her life on board slipping from her as she descended the gangway.

Warsing was waiting on the dock below. They walked to the hotel side by side. Making small talk with this man, it suddenly occurred to her that she didn't really know him. He asked after her family, but she didn't really know how they were. She'd called her father before she left Seattle—an awkward conversation full of clipped sentences and unspoken feelings that she was trying to forget. When they'd exhausted that fruitless line of questioning, he asked about her trip. Alice told him it was fine—she wasn't sure whether he wanted to know about the parties and the company of her fellow passengers. She followed him into the lobby and up a grand staircase. She wished for the minutes of uncomfortable conversation to speed by, but as they drew close to the hotel room, she wished they were slower. Fear ran cold down her spine, but she wasn't sure what she was afraid of.

The suite was large, extravagantly furnished and had a balcony facing the water. Warsing sat on the bed while Alice went out and gazed across the harbour. Down below, boats shuttled back and forth—sampans, ferries, and tall ships with sails that blew in the wind. They looked like illustrations from a pirate story. The distant hills were lush and steep, the city dense and bustling. The warm breeze smelled strange—everything was different—but she couldn't think about any of that. Her mind was preoccupied with the hotel room and the man who sat behind her. She looked out at the view as long as she could, her eyes flitting over every detail and taking in nothing at all. Eventually, she had to turn around.

Warsing beckoned for her to sit on his lap. He smelled like cologne and cigarettes, his shirt was smooth and white. His jacket was folded beside him, set aside with care. Alice was so close that she could see down his collar.

Suddenly, his lips were on hers, his hand on the back of her neck. He pulled her towards him so that their chests pressed together—he was everywhere around her. She pouted her lips, trying to match his movements. His mouth was wet, his tongue grazed her teeth. Her spine stiffened, she was a statue in his arms.

He pulled away. She avoided his eyes, looked down at her hands still rooted in place on her lap.

'You don't really want to kiss me, do you?' he said.

She shrunk into her chest, not knowing what to say. She didn't want to be rude, but she didn't want his mouth on hers again. 'No,' she said.

'So why do you?'

She expected him to be angry, but his brow was knitted, confused.

'Because you want me to,' she answered.

He frowned, lifted her off of his lap and ushered her towards an armchair on the other side of the room. He pulled a second armchair forward, sat, placed his hands on his knees and beckoned her to sit opposite him.

'Listen to me,' he said, his voice stern. 'Never do anything in your life unless you really want to.'

Her body loosened, her spine began to soften. She stopped worrying about the hotel room and started imagining the places that she might go next.

'Paris is the place for you,' Warsing went on. 'It's the only place for a talent like yours. But first, you should learn a little bit about your country.'

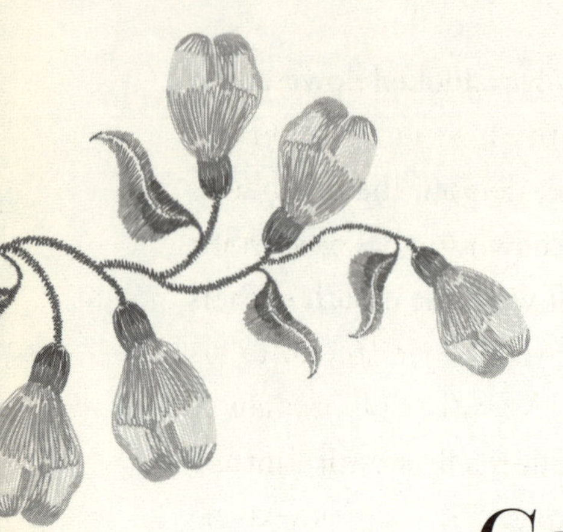

Canton

Alice had spent her entire childhood distinguished by being Chinese. It was the first thing people knew about her, the only detail they were sure to remember. Her age, her name, her interests—all of these things were secondary. But now that she was actually *in* Hong Kong, so close to her childhood home in Toishan, she couldn't have felt more American. Nothing was familiar, nothing was as she imagined. Everywhere she turned she encountered strange customs, foreign ideas—each moment was a discovery. It was exciting, at least, to be constantly surprised and the frustration she felt—at having been summoned to Hong Kong rather than Paris—soon gave way to exhilaration.

Her devout Christian parents never spent much time versing her in the spirituality of the country of her birth. Years of Sunday school had done nothing to acquaint her with the offering of fruit and gifts to long-deceased ancestors, the burning of incense, the worship of innumerable gods. She recognised the gravity of religion—there was a solemnity in the temples that she'd known in church back home—but in Hong Kong there was colour and celebration; a new world dipped in red and gold. Spirituality was everywhere—gods guarded doorways; auspicious colours, numbers and animals were painted on stores and homes. Her father's Christianity had never inspired Alice and she was equally sceptical of the faiths she encountered in Hong Kong, but she enjoyed the ritual and ceremony, the beautiful ornamentation. She tied ribbons to the wishing trees and prayed to the god of music for success in Europe.

She liked the density of the city—all of its insides spilling out onto the streets. Loud signs in Cantonese and English covered every surface. Cars, rickshaws, and carriages wove through narrow laneways, the old and the new crossed paths in the street. Thousands of years of history were rubbing up against the early 1930s. The British were everywhere—at times she felt as though she were in London. Stately buildings with row after row of columns and arches stood along the shoreline, the Union Jack hanging from their balconies. But it was the local culture that Warsing wanted her to experience. He took her to temples and ancestral halls, tranquil gardens and hidden restaurants. She saw the same remedies her father had used in his practice, tasted the same dishes her mother cooked at home. Everywhere they went, Warsing bought her gifts—blue-and-white porcelain, jewellery of jade and gold.

She dressed like the locals, in gauzy Chinese dresses that hugged her figure. When she passed white-American girls wearing slit skirts she thought that they looked foolish. The

British never wore Chinese dress, they were too busy playing pillars of society in the outposts of the Empire. When Alice walked the streets with Warsing, she noticed men's eyes flitting over her body—Warsing noticed too, drawing her close to his side.

They travelled along the Pearl River all the way up to Canton where they spent weeks exploring the port city and visiting his friends. It was Christmas of 1932, though she saw little sign of the western holiday on the streets of Canton. Although a native of Siam, it seemed Warsing had friends everywhere. The Sze-Yup dialect Alice's parents spoke at home was useless in the cities they visited, so Warsing was her voice and ears. Translating on her behalf, he enjoyed playing the expert tour guide.

She disliked following in his wake and was irked by his constant orders. She wanted to hurry on to Europe, to begin life as a violinist. Warsing wanted her to mind her manners, to be more patient, to have some respect for her culture and elders. She flirted with the idea of running off without him, but she had no means to get by on her own. She had to remain on the path she'd chosen.

Over time they made compromises, bent a little to each other's will. They continued to argue, but their debates were limited to literature and music, to philosophy, spirituality and social etiquette. Falling into a rhythm, she played the attentive student when he took her to historical sites; he played the captive audience when she practised the violin. He insisted that she rehearse daily and she was more than happy to oblige. Every night, she provided a recital, filling their hotel rooms with the music of Europe.

Indispensable

Workers hoisted a banner over the entrance to Redfern's industrial Carriageworks. Floodlights illuminated those five hallowed words, Mercedes Benz Fashion Week Australia. As daylight broke, the industry's elite flooded into the repurposed concrete halls. Inside, they sipped San Pellegrino and Peroni, getting well acquainted with the event's sponsors.

Those who hadn't received an invite, but wanted to be seen, paraded up and down the abandoned railyards, attracting photographers with the strategic implementation of glittered jackets and thigh-high boots. iPhones hoisted in the air, guests took as many photos as the official photographers, broadcasting proof that they were there.

These were just the trimmings—the main event was on the runway. There, Australia's most prominent designers, from Dion Lee and Strateas Carlucci to Carla Zampatti and Maticevski, presented their latest creations to those who were considered worthy spectators. Front and second row, in seats that had been reserved with Maja in mind, I sat and bore witness to the latest in Australian fashion history. In a blur of colour and light, my breath rose and fell to the beat of the model's footsteps, caught in the frenzied bliss of life at the eye of the zeitgeist.

I'd never been so excited to walk through a doorway than I was when I first entered the windowless concrete press room. Writers and photographers were crowded around long tables—sitting on yellow acetate chairs, typing frantically on laptops squeezed between potted ferns and decorative pineapples. Vibrant patterned rugs hung on the wall. There were deadlines to meet between shows, photos to upload and caption, emails to send. Throughout the week I rushed in and out of that room, the Flair logo printed on a piece of paper and taped to the table in front of my seat. I panicked about getting my work done in time and lived on overpriced sandwiches from the kiosk, but I never stopped pinching myself.

On Wednesday, my stiletto heel snapped right off. I hobbled eight blocks to a shoemaker in Redfern, sat on the footpath while my heel was repaired. I was covered in sweat, my makeup smeared by the time I made it back to Carriageworks. That night I sat at the Easton Pearson show, watching models pace up and down the runway in electric orange, khaki, royal blue, magenta—their beehive hairstyles and eyebrows painted equally bright. Shot silk suits and feathered dresses, beaded opera coats that would fit into Shan-Yi's wardrobe with ease. The collection was called

'Hyper Real' but it felt like a dream, my life had transitioned into a wonderland. When I arrived at the show a sequined scarf sat next to my name tag on the seat—as I watched I clung to the scarf, knowing that I'd keep it for the rest of my life. I was exhausted and I smelled disgusting, sweat was caked on my skin like a shell. I felt half delirious from the excitement and stress of the week—tears welled in my eyes, but I couldn't have been happier.

Then, Friday night came and the lights dimmed. As quickly as the crowds trotted in, they disappeared again. The clothes were wheeled out, the banners pulled down—it was all over for another year.

Back in the Flair office I realised how much I wanted to stay and prove myself to Maja. For years I had worked towards goals and come away with little to show for it. The thrill of hard work actually *paying off* was exhilarating. I didn't just want to be the best intern that Maja had right *now*, I wanted to be the best intern that she had *ever* had.

I could impress Holly by being a good assistant, by being organised and anticipating needs. But it would take something more to make an impact on Maja. I had to find a real way to contribute—to be of financial value to Flair. And the money at Flair was in beauty.

I never thought much about beauty products before I worked there. I spent money on them, but they never occupied much space in my mind. Makeup, haircare, and skincare were utilitarian—they served a purpose and that was that. Nothing to get excited about. But the women I met at product launches and events spoke to one another in the language of beauty. If I was going to succeed, I would have to learn their language.

I was always the only intern among the crowd of beauty writers and editors who represented other publications at events. While they attended events together all week long, I only saw them on the days I worked for Flair. When it came to making friends, I was starting out at a disadvantage—I was the random tag-along, the occasional interloper. Still I made conversation and smiled through my uncertainty.

The PR agents who played host to us writers always made it clear that we were part of an elite group. We were the in-crowd, the first in the know. The drinkers of cocktails and consumers of salad. Those who take photos of artisan pastries but do not actually eat them. You had to be somebody special to be invited to this place. The truth that we were nobody special at all was buried under the floristry and gift bags—the fact that few of us could afford the products we wrote about was never really mentioned. It was essential that we *feel* special, imperative that we arrive back at the office excited to tell the world what we'd seen.

The self-importance that grew from orbiting that world sparked off at events, in social-media feeds and then spread. The culture was one of silent one-upmanship. I was at the back of the pack and I could feel it—but it was only a tiny industry. The same thirty women at every single event. Small enough for me to see the women at the front and appreciate that they were trying to prove themselves just as much as I was. There was a certain prestige to working at a print magazine—at big names like *Vogue* and *Cosmopolitan*—but in the short time since I had started working at Flair, three major glossies had folded. The women I was surrounded by had fought to land their jobs, and I could see that even the leaders in the field were still fighting to keep them. I was glad to be working at an up-and-coming website. There was a security in knowing that I had nowhere to go but up.

The women I met wore formless black slips or clean-cut leather pencil skirts; each look indistinguishable from the last in a parade of minimal chic. Naturally pale skin was tanned all year round, never white or orange, but with an eternal sun-kissed glow. Except for the occasional splash of violent fuchsia lipstick, nobody stood out.

I began to notice new things about myself, more specific imperfections than I never noticed before. My photo was snapped in front of media walls, but never published anywhere. I didn't mind that—I wasn't there to be an Instagram starlet, and my name meant nothing to anyone—but I started to see myself differently.

I always knew that there was a commercial value to beauty, but I'd never really experienced it in person. Now, I could see how much it would help if I was a little less average. Would Shan-Yi have landed on her feet had she not been so beautiful? I felt shaky, but I tried to rise above my doubts. I compensated for my size-ten form (suddenly unacceptable) with higher-than-high heels and swinging trench coats. When the woman standing next to me introduced herself for the third time in a month, I pretended that I too couldn't remember that we'd met before.

I was sent home with beauty products every day and I

began to experiment with them, distinguishing between foundations and moisturisers that had previously appeared identical. I cleared out a cupboard to accommodate the goods and before long it looked like my own skincare store. I learnt about the science of anti-ageing skincare, about the appropriate technique for contouring. I pitched articles and videos, brainstormed ideas for competitions and subscription gifts. Some of my concepts were duds, and Maja never hesitated to tell me so—but others she liked and took on board. Soon she began to include me in more significant conversations, giving me greater responsibilities and encouraging me to write more content. I was making progress.

I was always on my best behaviour, always trying to sparkle, always looking my best. It took immense energy to play the part, it was exhausting to be the person that I was supposed to be. My cheeks ached from smiling.

Tom and I laughed about the work at Flair. The industry couldn't find a way to poke fun at its most absurd aspects—tongue was never in cheek at events—but with Tom I applied a healthy dose of sarcasm. I could say whatever I wanted and dress how I always dressed. It was like coming home from a foreign country—I enjoyed the relief of speaking my own language.

But our easy banter was interrupted by his wandering hands. A floodgate had been opened—he was always pulling at me, touching me. We were caught in a game of tag; he reached for my hand, I said 'no', and then we started all over again. Sometimes I thought that he liked it that way—there was a security for him in my turning him down. He didn't need to feel guilty because nothing would ever happen, my resistance was his safety net. And so the game carried on, a nuisance of poking and prodding.

I searched for a way to turn back the clock, to take my body off the table. We had a decade's history of successful friendship, of keeping our hands to ourselves. But despite my efforts, our friendship changed in the wee small hours of the morning, when the world was hazy and warm, seen through the syrupy gold of a wine glass. In those wandering hours, resistance grew exhausting, and I felt as though I was walking against the wind. That's when he would reach an arm around my waist, or brush a stray hair behind my ear. Occasionally he would slide his fingers between mine, and I wondered if it wouldn't be nice to leave them there. There was so much comfort to be derived from touching—I didn't have to be alone. I brushed him off as always, hissed 'stop' under my breath, but as time passed I started to doubt my own words.

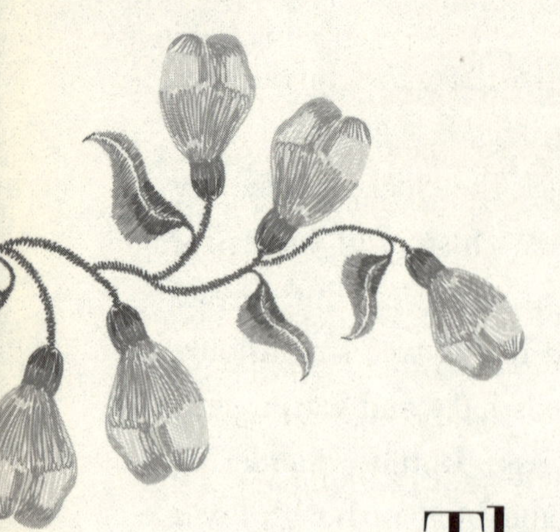

The Sage

When Warsing invited Alice to visit the sage he spoke as if he were asking for her hand in marriage. He had never addressed her with such reverence, pleading with his eyes as much as his words. She laughed—of course she would go with him. What choice did she have? He was the one keeping her alive and fed.

They set out on the Pearl River in a wooden sampan just big enough for the three of them—Alice, Warsing, and the vessel's owner, who sculled them along with a great curved oar. Alice found it funny to see Warsing squeezed into the rickety boat—Warsing with his taste for the finer things in life—but all morning a change had come over him. She had never known him to be humble: he was always the most intelligent, the most wealthy, the most important person in any room. But as he spoke to the owner of the sampan, he seemed to grow smaller and smaller, shrinking into himself. His behaviour and the swaying of the boat made Alice uneasy.

They passed islands of every size as they travelled downriver. Some were big enough to house entire districts of Canton, others were the size of a single village. As they drifted away from the heart of the city the river grew wide and untamed. There weren't as many fishing boats clustered along the shoreline, weren't as many people living on the water. The riverbanks became lush and wild. It was half an hour before they neared their destination: a tiny, barren island. Alice traced the outline with her eyes—just a small hill of sand and a jagged outcrop of rock. She turned towards Warsing in confusion.

'What on Earth is this?'

'Be quiet,' he said. 'Don't say a word.'

Climbing out of the boat, she lifted her skirt to step through the shallows to the shore. Appearing from nowhere, a small boy walked towards them, wearing the simple blue clothes that she often saw servants dressed in. She scanned the island, looking for some kind of shelter—the house from which this child had come—but there was nothing.

Alice was so preoccupied by the boy that she didn't see the sage until he was almost upon them. Walking a short distance behind the child, he was a sliver of a man, shrunken by age, with a wispy white goatee descending all the way down his chest. He wore a plain grey gown and his feet were bare. She had never seen anyone like him and yet she'd seen him hundreds of times before. He looked exactly like a picture from one of the Chinese textbooks she'd studied in Idaho.

The wizened man and the child stopped a few metres from the shore. Warsing placed his hand on Alice's back, urging her towards them. The sage addressed Warsing for around ten minutes and Alice listened with keen interest to the drum beat of his words, even though she couldn't understand them. When he finally turned to her, she instinctively lowered her gaze. He lifted her wrist, clasping it tightly between his bony fingers and gazed at the back of her hand for thirty seconds. Turning back to Warsing, the sage spoke for several minutes. When he finished, he and the child simply turned and walked away. There were no farewells, no formalities.

'Well,' Alice said. 'What was that all about?'

'Please,' hissed Warsing. 'Don't speak.'

Back in the sampan, a good distance from the island, Warsing finally broke the silence. There was bitterness in his voice. 'The sage said that you've come a long distance, that despite your youth you've travelled far.'

'Obviously I've come a long way if I don't speak the language.'

Warsing stared at her, his eyes gleaming. She could see that he believed the old man, even though he didn't like what he'd heard.

'You'll be married twice,' Warsing went on, shaking his head. 'Both times to Europeans, never to an Asian man. You'll have four children. You'll always be lucky in life—never rich, never poor—but in your middle years you'll be comfortably off. You'll live until you are ninety.'

Alice had never seen Warsing so sour and defeated. He was always so sensible, a man of intellect and wisdom. If she wasn't afraid of a reprimand she would have giggled at his faith. What a ridiculous thing to get upset about. If she didn't want to marry a European she wouldn't; if she didn't want four children she wouldn't have them. She was impressed with the sage—living on a barren sandbank, growing a storybook goatee—but if he had a magic power it was the gift of showmanship.

By the time they returned to the house in Canton, the old man and the child were already a distant memory.

Lingnan

Sometimes Warsing reminded Alice of her father. It didn't matter that he thought she was talented, it didn't matter that he wanted her to pursue the violin—the most important thing was that she have an education. In January of 1933 he wrote to Moscow High to request her academic transcripts and a recommendation for the University of Lingnan in Canton. She couldn't believe it when he enrolled her at the university and insisted that she remain there to study for three months and learn about her culture. *Three full months* more before she could get on her way.

Alice pleaded with him to reconsider—but there was only so much she could do, now that she'd placed her life in his hands. So she moved into a women's residence at the university and prepared to resume her schooling. While she studied, Warsing would attend to business and travel, and *then* they would make their way to Europe. He gave her pocket money to pay for weekend trips with her peers to Shanghai, Nanking and to Hong Kong, and encouraged her to embrace this chance to experience her country of birth. She took the money with begrudging thanks, no longer excited by the means to afford a solid meal.

Lingnan University stood on a vast island in the Pearl River. It was shady and serene, populated by broad-leafed trees and clusters of bamboo. There were tennis courts and athletic fields, the buildings were brown brick with glossy -green tile roofs, shaped like slanting bamboo. Originally founded by American missionaries, there was a strong western influence on campus and Alice was often reminded of the University of Idaho in Moscow. The students studied in English, so she was able to understand her classes and make friends. With Warsing's encouragement, she explored Canton. With friends she travelled to eat milk dessert at a popular tea room in Daliang, falling in love with the jelly-like milk. She liked the stained-glass windows and the dark-wood doors of Liwan, enjoyed watching craftsmen labour over pink-gold copper in the shade. She liked to watch the locals walking their birdcages through the streets, to listen to the chirping of birds as she drank her tea. She peered at the tiny birds in their cages, sitting happily on their swings. She wondered why they didn't squawk and cry or bat against the bars.

Alice wrote to her parents weekly about life in Canton. This narrow channel of communication remained between them, words folded with care into envelopes and posted across the globe. She worked to infuse her language with love, to send updates that demonstrated duty and respect. Her parents, busy with three small children and the grind of running a restaurant, only replied to a handful of her letters. But they kept her up to date on life in Ellensburg, sent detailed inquiries about her studies and her health.

However nice it was wandering around the city, she was frustrated at the university. This was not what she had left home for, not why she had travelled so far. If she was going to school, she might as well be back in the US. She was curt with her teachers, impatient in her classes. Her frustrations bubbled up inside her, beating against her skin. When she went to meet with the dean of women, who suggested that she behave in a more ladylike fashion, Alice was furious at the idea of being told how to conduct herself. She stormed out of the office and returned to her residence to pack up her things. Lingnan University was not where she belonged.

With plenty of pocket money in hand, she decided to go to Hong Kong. It wouldn't be long before Warsing would return to the city for business. Once they were reunited she could convince him to take her on to Paris.

Alone

I liked living alone. I liked coming home and finding my things exactly as I had left them—my food in the fridge, my dishes in the sink. I liked playing house, decorating and homemaking and cooking for myself. It didn't seem to matter how many years I had been living out of my parents' home, it felt like a game; I still felt like a child pretending to be a grown-up. I had survived the mould-infested horrors of a college residence hall and the diplomatic tangle of living in a share flat—finally having a place to myself felt like a luxury.

There were always fireworks going off over Sydney Harbour, explosions of purple and gold. Sometimes it would be a twenty-minute spectacle, funded by the Council; other times, just a stray sparkle, set off the back of a yacht. I would sit on the windowsill and watch, my legs hanging out into the inky abyss, the scent of smoke drifting into my bedroom.

I *liked* living alone, but there were moments when I wished there was somebody else about, somebody to shout out to—'Look at this!'

I asked around if anyone wanted to move into the apartment with me. I had the spare rooms, but nobody was tempted. None of my friends wanted to live among Shan-Yi's clutter in a suburb that was luxurious but quiet. I understood that. I would have felt the same way if it had been their apartment, if it had been their grandmother. Shan-Yi had lived alone for twenty years after her husband Andrew died. I wondered if she watched the fireworks over the water, if she enjoyed cooking for one and arriving home to the silence.

I was surrounded by souvenirs of her sex life. In the master bedroom there was a shelf of sex books, from classics like *The Kama Sutra* and *The Joy of Sex* to anachronistic titles such as *The Secrets of Making Love to Oriental Women*. In her desk drawer, I found a handful of keyrings. From each ring hung a naked man and woman—their plastic bodies could be fitted together by way of holes and pegs in the mouth and groin. A long Japanese scroll curled away on a bookshelf, the leathery paper covered in graphic sexual scenes, painted in dreamy watercolours. The apartment was charged with the intimate moments that the walls and curtains, the sculptures and paintings had witnessed.

My own sex life was non-existent, as confined to memory as hers. My days were full, my nights exhausted—but in the darkness, my mind was possessed by thoughts of what might be. I wished for somebody to fill the space around me. It was in the tossing and turning of early morning that I started to see things differently. There were thoughts that only came to mind in the humming silence of three am—admissions that were too raw to consider by day. In that early hour, I was stuck on a single memory—one with the power to block out guilt or anger. I could see it in cinematic colour, feel it on the tips of my fingers. The concern in Tom's face as he arched over me on the couch, the warmth of his hands as he tucked the blanket in around my shoulders. The feeling of his nose as it grazed against mine, the worry in his voice—'I don't want you to kill yourself.' A moment of believing that somebody cared.

Once I let that feeling in I couldn't let it go.

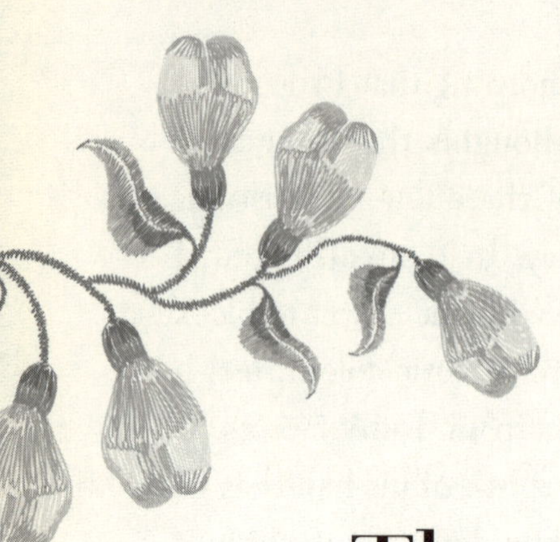

The German

Karl August Maier was twenty-five years old, and his twenty-fifth year had been his best so far. It was a year of travel as he seized the opportunity to explore the world before he was to marry his fiancée back in Thüringen. The trouble was, the more he travelled, the less he wanted to go home. He wondered if he would return at all, or if he would send for Erika to meet him somewhere abroad. There was still so much left to see.

In every country, Karl met foreigners who were eager to hear from a German. In Yaffa, Palestine, he had been invited to give a speech at the German Club. The expat community wanted a first-hand account of what progress the Nationalist-Socialist Party was making in the Fatherland. After that, he spent six months living as a subject of the British Empire in India. The British influence was powerful and the locals were fascinated by the news he brought. But it wasn't all about politics—he was no politician, after all, just a young man eager to dip his toes into every curiosity the world had to offer. His letters home grew longer and longer, providing vibrant accounts of everything he saw. Erika said that when he returned she would collect them together and have them published.

He wrote that at four o'clock on 14 April 1931, when he entered a cinema in Valencia, Spain, it had been an ordinary afternoon. At seven, when he emerged, the streets were full of banners and flags, girls dancing with ribbons of red, yellow and pink braided through their hair, and cheers of 'Viva la Republica!' that carried on until dawn—the Spanish republic was born. In Egypt, he had been arrested the moment he stepped off the boat in Alexandria, mistaken for a different Karl Maier. In India, he turned down proposals of marriage from the daughters of a Maharajah.

Karl wrote almost every day, though Erika, young, restless and preoccupied with petty troubles, was rarely able to pen a satisfactory response. When Karl spent a week in Genova, Italy, she mistook his locale for Geneva, Switzerland, and begged him to make the short journey home. He patiently explained that he had no intention of hurrying back to Thüringen—if only she read his letters, she would understand. He sympathised with her impatience, she was still just a child. Her words were clumsy, but they were brimming with sweetness. He and Erika understood each other, and they understood the expectations of the life they would build together. The world was full of temptation, but eventually Karl knew that he would return to his fiancée.

*

It was as if Alice was shedding skins, discarding a version of herself each time she left one place and arrived in the next. In Hong Kong, she was alone once again, but she was not the same person who she had been in Seattle. She wasn't on show any anymore she no longer had the sense that watchers followed wherever she went. She was part of Hong Kong and disappeared into the crowd.

It didn't hurt that she had money. In the afternoons she went for tiffin, in the evenings she ventured out to tea dances at the roof-top garden of the Hong Kong Hotel. The tea garden was as intimate as a club, and she grew to know all the regulars there, by face, if not by name. She sat and gossiped with other young women, grew proud and conscious of the beauty that made her stand out among her peers. Learning to leverage her charm, she tormented the young men she met—students at engineering and medical schools preoccupied with ideas of 'doing something for China'; graduates looking for work in the city; businessmen seeking a night of pleasure.

Newcomers were conspicuous at the hotel and she noticed Karl from the first. A handsome young German, seated alone—she sought him out to dance. He had a steady hand, guiding her across the floor with ease; his eyes were the most startling blue. At the end of the night, she accepted an invitation to dinner. When she returned to her room her thoughts were full of him. Rummaging through the wardrobe, she pulled out her American dresses and evening gowns, abandoned since her arrival in Hong Kong. When she arrived for dinner in her beaded black dress, he swung her into a deep kiss.

They met several times that week and she drew away from her other new friends. Karl worked for a New York based publishing company and was funding his travel by selling magazines and journals. A talented salesman, he contracted stockists and subscribers in every corner of the globe. He told her about his business, about his home back in Germany, and was honest with her from the start. He told her about his fiancée back in Thüringen, that they were 'betrothed', a kind of commitment that was more serious than the typical engagement. He was perfectly clear with Alice that there could never be anything serious between them. But he wanted to see her every day. Before she knew it, she wanted to see him every day too.

Their conversations were different from any that she'd ever had before. Their words came faster and faster, as though they were trying to race each other to a finish line. But the finish line never came, there was always more to say. She delighted in disarming him. He was so sure of himself and so direct in his opinions—when Alice arrived for dinner one evening with a handkerchief in hand, coughing and sniffling, he didn't bother to coddle her.

'I've known plenty of silly girls,' he said, 'but even the greatest fool knows that if she marches around town every evening without so much as a shawl on she's going to fall ill. Have you been to the doctor?'

'No,' she confessed. 'It's just a cold.'

'Go,' he replied. 'And when you do, have the doctor check your head while he's at it—ask him to see if that pea-sized brain of yours is still rattling around in there.'

He swooped in to kiss her, laughing and scrunching his

face to suggest he was repulsed by her sniffling.

'I might be a fool,' she said when he released her, 'but I'm the fool I choose to be. I'll go where I like and wear what I like and won't take any medical advice from a big-headed salesman who thinks he's a doctor.'

Whenever she retaliated she could see him tilting off balance. The more she challenged him the more closely his eyes followed her, so she sharpened her tongue and was quick to speak. Before long, when they went out at night, she could tell that she was the only woman he could see. The thrill of it scorched right through her.

Karl called her *Schnitz*, Little One. His arm stretched across her back as they walked the streets, seeing her safely home—he was her protector. They sat and smoked on the balcony of his hotel room—their backs against the wall, the fur rug from the divan pulled around them in a soft heap—and watched the sun go down and the shadows crawl up the hillsides, lights glimmering in the neighbouring villas. Alice began to depend on the warmth of his chest, the graze of his cheek against hers. With each week that passed she thought of him more and thought less about his betrothal. It wasn't long before it crossed her mind that she might be in love.

For a while she kept him a secret, but when her benefactor returned to Hong Kong, she was forced to confess. Warsing was enraged and immediately severed her allowance, insisting that if she stayed with 'that foreign tramp' she would have to get by on her own. It was all or nothing—Karl or Warsing.

As far as Alice was concerned, the choice was easy.

Collision

The days were growing cooler, the nights began to close in. I always seemed to miss out on summer—it slipped by before I could remember to make time to go to the beach. As an adult, working one job or another, I didn't have time for the season in the way I had done as a child. I didn't succumb to the sweaty, salty mess of it—I was passive smoking summer.

All my summer memories seemed to belong to childhood. They were memories of cousins and sandy beaches and long rides home with red hot skin. Of tactical manoeuvres honed in games of Marco Polo, played in backyard pools. Of Bubble O'Bills and Golden Gaytimes and Splices, of white-hot panic when heartless 'Back to School' slogans replaced Christmas ornaments in all the shop windows.

The best days of summer were the ones spent at Nielsen Park. On the hottest of days, Mum would bundle me and

Tristan into the car and make the long drive across Sydney. At the shady beachside park, we would stretch out across picnic rugs with family and friends, spend the day in and out of the harbour. Eating wide orange slices from tupperware containers and vegemite sandwiches wrapped in glad wrap. Once, we built sandcastles big enough to sit in. Another time, in an unusual fit of athletic fervour, I swam laps along the shark net, back and forth until nightfall. When I finally emerged from the water, fingers and toes shrivelled, half a dozen jelly blubbers fell out of my board shorts.

As the last warm days of summer were eaten up by my internship at Flair, I wanted something to hold on to, so I lined up a Friday night outing: fish and chips on the beach at Nielsen Park. Friends, including Tom, travelled across Sydney by bus in a race against the setting sun and we sat on the rocks in the dusty light, eating with our hands. Sand and salt blended together, hair battering our faces, darkness closing in. But we didn't care—everything tastes delicious when your feet are dipped in the cool of Sydney Harbour.

Later, I piled as many friends as I could fit into my car and drove them home to the Inner West. By the time we got to Summer Hill we were all keen for a drink, so we went to my parents' house, vacant while Mum and Dad spent a weekend down the coast. Soon it was just Tom, Ryan and me, surrounded by empty bottles of beer and cider.

As the night grew old, Ryan drifted off to sleep. It had been a long time since Tom and I were alone, lying there together on the living-room floor. The house was dark and dizzy. The gravitational pull between us was tugging everything inwards, squeezing the whole world into the space between us. Before long there was no space left. He was pulling me towards him, planting kisses all over my face—everywhere but on my lips.

Again we were at that pivotal moment—the point when I pulled away and said no. But I didn't *want* to say no, I didn't *want* him to stop. I let him cling to me, as though the fact that I wasn't kissing him back excused my behaviour. As though inaction were an acceptable excuse for allowing a friend's boyfriend to run his hands all over my chest. His fingers slid down into my underwear, finding their way between my legs. He let out a great sigh and looked me straight in the eyes; I leant forward and kissed his cheek.

It was as though the touch of my lips sent a bolt of electricity right through him. As though the moment I acted, the fantasy came crumbling down. He pulled away, releasing me. He was up and out of the room in moments.

He stopped in the kitchen and poured himself a glass of water. 'This isn't good,' he said, his eyes wild and searching. 'This can't happen again.'

'I know.'

He made his way down the hallway and out onto the street.

'Wait,' I said. 'Stay.'

'I can't be around you anymore,' he snapped. 'No texting, no anything. This is done.'

He was gone before I could reply.

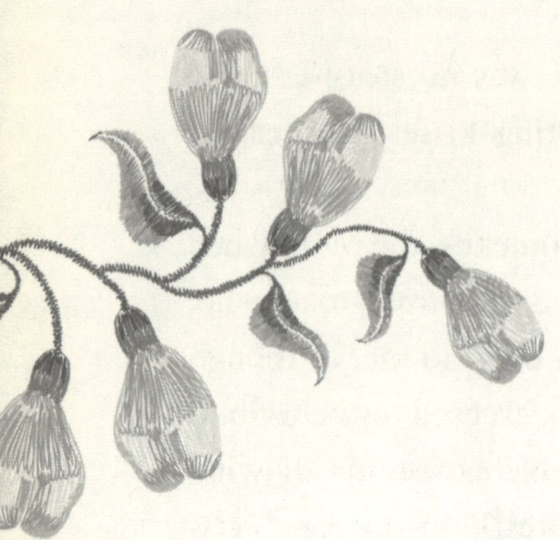

Reunion

In the summer of 1933, Yee Lee decided his youngest children—Cora, Sammy, and Bob—were becoming too American. It was time they developed a sense of where they came from. The school year was over, so he and Poon Wong packed up the restaurant and made arrangements to move the family back to China; stopping first in Hong Kong.

When Alice received news by letter that her parents and younger siblings would be visiting, she held her breath for word that they wanted to see her. It was just over a year since she had left America, but it felt like a lifetime. She invited them to her favourite restaurant near the harbour. Her siblings were visiting their parents' part of the world, but to Alice, who had started a life in Hong Kong, it felt as though her parents were coming to visit *hers*. There was a thrill in taking a far-off place and slowly making it her own—she was proud of the city and delighted when they accepted her dinner invitation. She took time over her hair, scrubbed under her fingernails and polished her shoes. She remembered the lessons her mother and father had taught her, lessons she hadn't considered in all the time she'd been away. It was the first night she had spent without Karl in weeks. As she walked towards the restaurant, she felt his absence beside her. It was as though she had left her purse at home—something important was missing. But it wasn't just Karl's absence—she felt strange all over. At a familiar intersection she took the wrong turn. She tried to calm herself but her palms were sticky with sweat.

Her family was waiting for her outside the restaurant and her mother burst into tears as soon as she saw her. Alice didn't know where to look as her parents took turns hugging her. She couldn't meet their eyes. Cora had shot up to almost her mother's height—her little sister was now eleven years old. Her two brothers were no longer babies but energetic children, climbing all over her as the family sat down to eat dinner. She hooked Bob under her arm, bouncing him up and down as she devoured her roast duck. The more the children laughed and played, the more she was able to find her words. She offered anecdotes like peace branches, drawing her parents into her world.

'I never imagined you would come this far,' said Yee. 'I never thought you would make it to Seattle.'

'He was certain you'd be back,' said Poon Wong. 'Absolutely certain that you'd return home in a week.'

Her mother's eyes were glossy but she buried her head

in her meal, her lips pursed. A new feeling pierced Alice's chest, a specific kind of regret she hadn't felt before.

'I'm impressed,' said Yee. 'Despite the choices you've made, I'm impressed how far you've come on your own. But what will you do next?'

He looked at her directly, the question an accusation. Alice didn't know what to say.

'Are you playing the violin? Are you working as a musician?' he asked.

She thought of her violin lying in its case, tucked safely under the bed in her hotel room. She hadn't touched it since first meeting Karl.

'There's no reason for you to be in Hong Kong,' Yee said sternly, though his eyes were soft. 'We'll pay your fare back to America, you can live with Marie and Mi. Go to the University of Idaho, go back to your Professor Claus. You need an education.'

Alice felt as if she were a small child again, sitting with her siblings at the kitchen table.

She spent the next week showing her brothers and sister the towering coils of incense in Hong Kong's temples, took them for walks along the harbour foreshore, filled them up with ice cream and crumbling custard tarts. As for the idea of playing hostess to Yee and Poon Wong, it disintegrated as soon as they stepped out together onto the bustling streets. Her parents were instantly locals, speaking the language, familiar with the customs —she was *their* guest.

Alice had intended to tell them about Karl, but the

conversation seemed impossible and the relationship soon morphed into a guilty secret. She couldn't tell them that he would never marry her, couldn't tell them that he would soon be returning to Germany. How could she describe this man to her father? This beautiful blond man, almost a decade her senior. This charming, intelligent, compassionate man who refused to make her his wife.

There was another reason she felt nervous to introduce her parents to the man she loved; during the long nights they had spent together, Karl talked about politics and told her stories about Germany as they sat in the candlelight. Alice didn't care for politics and his words wouldn't have worried her had it not been for Warsing, who was angry at the rise of a noxious movement in Germany whose thugs were bullying their way into power. Alice would never forget the vitriol in his voice as he spoke about Germans—but his words did not apply to Karl. Karl was as wise as Warsing; Karl knew what he was about.

Still, Alice kept her love a secret, carried it silently in her heart.

When it came time for her family to leave Hong Kong and head on to the mainland, she was as surprised as anyone when she announced she would be going home to Moscow.

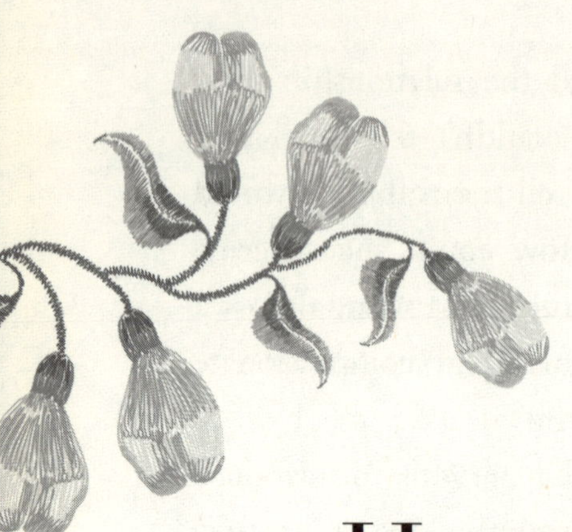

Homecoming

The University of Idaho was as sprawling and green as ever, but it wasn't quite the same. Now eighteen, Alice was finally old enough to belong on campus, but something about belonging made the place seem ordinary. Returning to Moscow and enrolling felt like being ripped from a fairyland to discover everything just as it had been.

She was glad to be back studying with Professor Claus in his office: this was the room where all of her dreams were born. Professor Claus had also just returned to Moscow, having spent the summer of 1932 studying advanced conducting and musical literature at the Salzburg Orchestral Academy in Austria. Spending time with esteemed conductors had made him even more passionate and serious about his music, meanwhile Alice had barely touched her violin in months. He was appalled by the state of her playing and did not hesitate to criticise her technique.

After the family reunion in Hong Kong, Alice's parents and three younger siblings had travelled on to Canton and through a web of tiny villages to see extended family. They then went north to Nanking, where her father invested in a block of apartments and the family settled down. Back in Moscow, Alice moved in with her eldest sister and brother-in-law, Marie and Mi. The couple, married almost three years, were busy making a living at The Grill. Alice worked at the restaurant for just a few hours each day, but Marie and Mi rose before the sun and worked until well after midnight. When Alice came home to an empty house she practised the violin until her shoulders ached and her eyes were tired.

She was allowed to go where she pleased as long as she continued to work at The Grill and attend to her studies. She was much more an adult than when she last lived in Moscow, but much more a child than she had been in Hong Kong. Sometimes she felt her entire year abroad only existed in her imagination. If that was the case, the daydream lingered on.

She managed to stay in Idaho for five months, trying to embrace college life, but it wasn't long before the outside world beckoned. She gave Karl her Moscow address when she farewelled him in Hong Kong, but hadn't heard a word from him until he wrote to her from Calcutta. He said that he had travelled back to India where he'd had success as a salesman, but contracted a near-fatal case of typhoid and spent three months in hospital. The shocking reminder of his mortality forced him to reassess his life—a betrothal might be important, but Alice was even more so.

He begged her to come to India.

Mi and Marie were down-to-earth people, sensible in business and practical in life. They could see that Alice would never be appeased by Moscow. She was too romantic, too strong-willed—it was pointless to try to tame her. Putting aside their reservations, they met her determination with love and paid for her passage back across the oceans. Professor Claus was exasperated, but he too realised the decision had been made.

Mi and Marie stood with her at the bus stop on the edge of the University of Idaho campus, her single suitcase at their feet. The sun was barely up, the morning air biting as they waited, unable to find words to address the reality that Alice might never return.

'Thank you.' Alice eventually broke the silence. 'Thank you for letting me go.'

Marie didn't acknowledge her sister's words, instead she dropped her head and began to riffle through her purse. Drawing out sixty dollars, she placed the notes in Alice's hand, folding her palm over them.

'This will protect you if anything goes wrong. Keep it for an emergency.'

Bombay

On 27 November 1935, when Alice and Karl married, the Calcutta heat was unrelenting. Their hotel room felt like a warm bath. They were woken, as always, by the blinding sun bouncing off the harbour—their balcony was so close to the Indian Ocean that they took turns trying to spit cherry pits into its depths. They didn't care that the pits fell down onto the road below, didn't see that they could never reach the water. The onion domes and gothic flourishes of the Taj Mahal Palace Hotel towered just out of reach, the Gateway of India monument stood in clear view.

'That's where all the British viceroys and governors pass,' said Karl, pointing down to the yellow basalt arch. 'To make their ceremonial entrance to the realm.'

'Let's come back here,' said Alice. 'When we've earned some money. Let's come back and stay at the Taj, and remember today—remember what it was like when we first came here together.'

'You're spoiled, Schnitz,' he said. 'We may never make that kind of money.'

'Then let's come and stay here, or sleep in the park. I want to be here again with you.'

They took a taxi to the registration office, with its old-fashioned pigeon holes and the smell of ancient paper. There was no formal ceremony, no friends present, just the civil servant who bound them together for life. They were impatient to be married and they hurried through the paperwork. It was done within half an hour, the taxi waiting outside.

They had their wedding lunch at Carnegie's, where life carried on exactly as usual—an ordinary afternoon—with guests lingering over lunch in the refreshing cool of the restaurant. But the band boys knew Alice and Karl and they struck up a love song just for the two of them. The newlyweds grinned in delight, thrilled by the obliviousness of everyone else.

Alice was a German wife now, so she spelled her name in the German way—the way that Karl liked it—Alys Virginia Maier. She would never be Alice again. Alys inherited lessons in marriage from her mother and found herself reflecting on words taught to her since birth. Her rebellious nature quietened. As a wife she was entering a new world—taking not only her husband's name, but his family, beliefs and loyalties.

She travelled from country to country by her husband's

side, with her new German passport in hand. In October of 1937, two years after their marriage, he took her to meet his parents. She expected they would travel to Thüringen—but as a mixed-race couple they were no longer welcome there. They met Karl's family—his mother, father, and brother Hans—in Rome instead. The Maiers had grown to love Karl's former fiancée, Erika; they remembered the many afternoons they spent with her, sharing their son's letters over cake. *They* had been the ones to witness her tears when Karl had broken off the engagement. But this new foreign girl seemed as kind as she was quick-witted—and she charmed them. Karl's father in particular took to Alys and came to treat her like a daughter. She walked arm in arm with her father-in-law, down the Via del Corso.

From the time that they were married, Karl and Alys travelled and worked together. They were both sales representatives for the Union Circulation Company, selling subscriptions to *Harper's Bazaar* and *News of the World* throughout Asia. From India they travelled through Malaysia, the Philippines, and then back to Hong Kong. There was something special about being in the city where they'd first fallen in love. Every street was paved with its own set of memories. She was full of newlywed bliss—the high of being by Karl's side and the agony of separation when they were apart. Whenever he went out for drinks with his friends, she curled up in the hotel window and watched the lights reflecting across the harbour. Her mind was busy with thoughts of Karl, waiting for him to come home. She looked through his books—Flaubert, Dostoevsky, Nietsche, *Fundamentals of Salesmanship*, a volume of card tricks, encyclopaedias and dictionaries—she always felt that she could tell so much about a person from their books. Other times she wrote poetry and stories. She wrote about herself in third person, wove flowery narratives about her time with Karl—stories about her life that differed from reality, but weren't completely fiction either.

When Karl stayed out into the morning hours she never went to bed. Waiting at the window she wondered where he was. She hoped that he missed her as much as she missed him. When loneliness and worry encroached she brushed them aside—she chose instead to bask in love.

Not long after they were married, Alys received a letter from her father in Nanking. Her seven-year-old brother Sammy was dead, the second of her brothers to be taken by spinal meningitis. For all the time she had spent away from her family, she never felt so lonely as she did when she read that letter. She mustered up memories of Sammy in Moscow, running between her legs while she played the violin. But the memories were hazy and incomplete. She barely knew him. They were four siblings now—Marie, Alys, Cora and Bob—each at least than six years apart from the next. She wondered how many of her family would die as strangers. But *they* all knew each other, it was *she* who was apart, she who was out adrift in the world. That night in bed, she buried her face into Karl's neck, holding him closer than ever before.

After Sammy's death, she found herself thinking more and more of her own family, the one she would start with Karl. She repeatedly dreamed of babies and toddlers of varying shapes and sizes, always tight in her arms. She was startled, alarmed by the urgency of such grown-up reveries. She was only nineteen, but had turned into an adult without even noticing.

Karl had begun taking long walks alone in the evenings; when he was home, he busied himself with dull things, and if she dared to interrupt him with a kiss or caress, she saw impatience in his upwards glance. She consoled herself that it meant nothing; men were different; they preferred comrades to lovers in the daytime. That was incomprehensible to her, but if he wished it so, she would make it so for him.

As years passed, Karl and Alys settled into married life—but even so, her first pregnancy arrived too soon. They were citizens of the world, untethered wanderers—Karl wasn't prepared to give that up.

'We can't travel with a baby,' Karl said. 'We can't do our work, we can't live our lives.'

'Please,' she said, tears welling up in her eyes. 'It might not be the perfect time, but this happened for a reason.'

'We have no home,' he argued, resolute. 'What kind of life is this for a child? You're being selfish.'

He took her to the doctor's office. They could be parents when they were older.

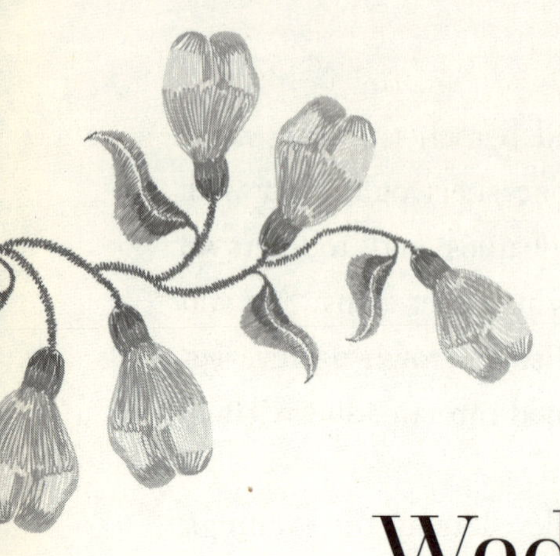

Wednesday Afternoon

'We're going to miss you when you're gone.' Maja was sifting through bags of lip gloss when she said those words, late on a Wednesday afternoon near the end of my internship. We were discussing ideas for a series of fitness articles, reviewing new trends from Pilates at the barre to working out with weighted drumsticks.

'You're our best little volunteer.'

The conversation charged on, as it always did. We continued to dissect the merits of combining styles of yoga, of singing karaoke during spin class. I offered suggestions for posts and laughed at stupid trends—but I was distracted by the forceful thump of my heart against my chest. There was no position for me at Flair.

On my last day Maja gave me lipsticks and perfume, a glass skull of vodka that had been gifted to the team. With a hug and a kiss, we said our goodbyes, offering one another best wishes and thankyous. Maja talked about the freelance pieces that she planned to have me contribute; said that I would be their first point of call if ever a full-time position arose. But the fact was, they just couldn't afford anyone right now.

I sent résumés to websites and magazines, but the weeks that followed my departure from Flair were a waiting game, punctured by cover letters that evoked no response. I had a sense of purpose when I was working at Flair—not a social or creative purpose—but of having a project that needed to get done. Now I was back to being unemployed and confused, trying to convince strangers to take a chance on me.

One ache fed another. Despite all the parties that I threw in the apartment, the space between my friends and I had grown much wider than the distance between the Eastern Suburbs and the Inner West. They were there in my home each day—their photos, their updates, their news posted online—but they were always just out of reach. Like my favourite characters on TV, their lives filled mine with laughter and intrigue. But they couldn't be touched, couldn't be held.

In a whole year I hadn't been able to mend the fractures that I inflicted on my friendships during a few months of depression and withdrawal. During high school and university—when our lives travelled in parallel—friendship had been a foregone conclusion. My friends just *were*; our group just *was*. Now, having friends was something that I had to schedule and work at, like exercise or eating a healthy diet. It was exhausting and laborious, and I couldn't find a shortcut.

I wondered if the internship had hurt my social life, if filling my social media with glamorous pictures had given the impression that I had better things to do. Perhaps my friends thought I was off on an adventure rather than sitting at home, wishing for an invite to the local pub. I wondered if they knew how much I missed them.

Tom was true to his word; we hadn't spoken in ages. At social events he skirted around me—where before we would whisper to one another, tell inside jokes and laugh—now we stood on opposite sides of the room. If I handed him a drink he accepted it arching backwards, as though I were contagious. I was disappointed in myself, embarrassed by the choices that had led to the loss of my friend. But I was angry with Tom too, pissed off that I was the one cast out on her own. He had been the one to instigate the change between us—now he was off with Jessica, while I was down a confidante. Darkness began to creep in from behind me.

My parents were supportive; my mum was my closest friend. She cared so much and so deeply, I could see that every hurt I felt was her hurt too. She came round often and we watched *Gilmore Girls* together on Shan-Yi's velvet settee or walked down to Rose Bay for burgers and milkshakes. But I couldn't let her carry my heavy feelings.

I returned to exploring Shan-Yi's apartment. I ventured into the storeroom, into the piles of paperwork. The room smelled like a musty old library and you couldn't touch anything without your hands becoming coated in some strange invisible grime. Shan-Yi had carefully catalogued and labelled everything—records, photo albums, and reels of sixteen-millimetre film—but the system made no sense. Captions were written with assumed knowledge in mind, notes had been left that could only be deciphered by their author. I found copies of Karl's travel journals, a pile of passports and an album of assorted newspaper clippings. A torn extract from *The Sunday Sun & Guardian* dated 20 November 1946 exclaimed that, 'Soignee-black-suited Shan-Yi Lee, whose charm is as infectious as a baby's smile, made ageing hearts beat madly when she toed the red carpet at lunch-time at Prince's.' I found ornate certificates from Qantas and Pan Am congratulating her and her second husband Andrew for crossing the equator, which they did often enough to lose any sense of occasion. There was a mention in the *Guinness Book of World Records* that the 'Longest airline ticket ever issued was one measuring 33 feet long issued in June 1957 to Mr & Mrs Andrew Balogh of Sydney for a journey taking in 33 countries, 105 cities and using 28 airlines.'

I found box after box of letters, many with multiple carbon copies, written on a daily basis and sent around the world. The pages had turned caramel brown and were wrinkled; some of the ink was faded, while other words stood out bold and clear. As a result, the letters looked like they were written in a secret code—as though the bold words could be threaded together to reveal a hidden message.

I read Shan-Yi's letters in my spare time, but after several weeks I had only managed to get through a handful of the countless pages. There were too many to manage and the pages were too disjointed and strange: vivid scenes peppered with countless gaps, days narrated in intricate detail without context or explanation. I guessed the recipients required no clarification—they truly knew her.

If I hadn't begun to ask questions about Shan-Yi's life, I might never have even known about the video. It had been sitting there for years, on a USB in my father's study, but it was only when I asked Dad about her that he told me it existed. It was made more than a decade before Shan-Yi's death, when Dad sat her down in front of a camera and asked her to tell him her life story. 'I have nothing interesting to tell,' she said when he first made the request. But soon she was as invested as he was, calling to arrange a date to film and tolerating his fussing over angles and lighting. When I asked him for a copy, Dad handed me the USB as though it was nothing at all. In contrast, I carried the drive home as though it was the most precious thing in the world. My heart raced as I waited to hear what she had to say. Plugging it into my laptop, I lay back on her settee to watch.

'I was born in China in 1916, and in 1920, I went with my mother and my older sister to America to join my father, who sent for us at that time. It was just after the finish of the First World War...'

She is sitting in the living room of her apartment, leaning back in an armchair, cooling herself with a red paper fan. Her hair is white, she's in her eighties but she's plump and healthy—not the frail little woman that I remembered from the end. Her eyebrows are tattooed on, a choice she made when she grew tired of pencilling them in each day. Artificial cherry blossoms extend from a vase and reach behind her shoulder. Though she pauses to remember details and dates, she speaks with a steady directness, in the accent which I suppose was mostly American but just sounded like Shan-Yi to me. The same matter-of-fact woman that I knew—aware that her story was fascinating but brushing it off as nothing. It is what it is, it was how it was. She talks about her life in great sweeps and bounds, an extraordinary story trimmed down to ninety minutes.

'I knew nothing; I didn't know how babies came. Can you imagine that? At sixteen. Normally, there's so much whispering and giggling between girls at that age at school, that you have a pretty good idea about things. I had no idea about anything. But I did know, that if I was going to be taken to a doctor, that he was accusing me of something very bad...'

My hair stood on end as her voice filled the room, so real and clear and vibrant. As I listened to her words, the gaping holes in her story began to fill up with information. It was like turning to the answer page at the back of a maths textbook—much of what I needed was right there all along.

But the new information had holes in it too. I was frustrated by the questions that my father didn't ask—exasperated by his incurious response to her tales.

Throughout the video she made baffling statements that begged for follow-up questions. Some things she said made no sense to me at all. I wanted to reach into the screen and shake my father—to step into the past and insist that she clarify.

The video was captivating and infuriating; I was thrilled to have so many answers, delighted by the new picture of Shan-Yi's life that lay out before me. But the feeling was short-lived. By the time I finished watching, I had more questions than I started with.

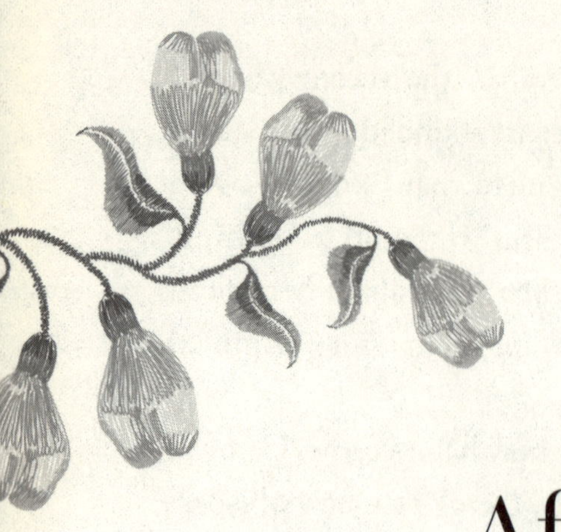

Africa

Alys and Karl travelled as though they were playing a game of tag. Karl typically went ahead to get things settled, and Alys followed behind, joining him when he sent word. His was the steady arm to guide her—forever protecting her from the hazards of travel. In 1937, they decided to spend a full year in Africa where they could continue to sell magazine subscriptions while exploring a new corner of the world. Lying in their bed in Hong Kong, legs intertwined, they spun romantic tales of the adventures that they would share on safari.

Alys was to travel from Hong Kong to meet Karl in Mombasa, Kenya, where his boat would make a stop on its way down the east coast of the continent. But before she left she received a telegram from Karl warning her that there were Nazis on board the ship, impatient for a fight. This was no place for a German man to show off his Chinese wife. It was better that she join him in Tanzania at the port in Dar es Salaam. She enjoyed being precious to Karl, the thing that he cared about most in the world. But it seemed that being safe often meant being alone.

After Tanzania, they went through South Africa—to Durban, Cape Town, and finally to Johannesburg, where they agreed to stay for six months. While on the move they were bound together, united by the thrill of new people and places. It was when they were stationary and settled down that Alys felt the greatest space between them. When they slowed down, life sped up, its ordinariness threatening to stifle them.

They made friends in Johannesburg, spent afternoons watching the summer storms and drinking into the evening. Alys often went to bed early, but she could never fall asleep until Karl was home to join her. Anxiety encroached on her mind. She lay awake worrying about where he was and what he was up to. The fear filled her with energy, the energy kept her from sleep. She could feel herself losing touch with reality.

When Karl came home, she could taste the alcohol seeping from his pores. She smothered him with kisses, but he pulled away. The less he wanted her, the more she wanted him. She grew stifling and impossible. She often thought of Erika, the fiancée who had been a burden to Karl. Now, Alys was becoming a burden, she was the nagging responsibility that her husband couldn't escape. She contorted her emotions, forcing herself back into the woman he had married.

'You've been with another woman,' she snapped, when he came home one night with lipstick smeared across his cheek. 'Don't lie to me. I'm not stupid.'

'Tonight you are being very stupid,' he said. 'You think that because some fool kissed my cheek it means that I've been unfaithful. Your imagination is going to destroy this marriage.'

'It's three in the morning,' she said, unable to stop the tears that were sliding down her cheeks, 'where have you been?'

'If you loved me the way I love you, you would trust me,' argued Karl. 'I've given you all I have to give.'

There was the other argument too. The one that followed them across the oceans, that stood between them wherever they went. They had been in Johannesburg for so long, could this be where they might raise a child? But Karl didn't want a baby. For months he said it was because of their location—we won't be here long enough, we don't have a real home—but she argued and argued until he confessed the truth—this was no time for a mixed-race child, not in South Africa, not in this world.

Alys wept at his words, clutching him tight and begging him to reconsider. She trusted that he knew the world better than she did. New fears crept in to plague her, fears that Karl was right.

When their time in South Africa was done she was glad. Five years of travelling with Karl had taught her that there was always a fresh start to be had on the other side of an ocean. They were going on to Australia, things would be better there.

Sydney

On 1 June 1938, Karl and Alys disembarked from the steam liner SS *Oronsay* in Sydney, Australia. After spending several months in the city, they travelled on to Melbourne and Adelaide, selling subscriptions wherever they went. But their breathtaking arrival to Sydney by boat lingered on their minds, and a year later they returned to the city, with its eternal harbour stretching outward before them. There, Karl and Alys spent long days out on the water, emerald headlands looming above, secreting them away. Stretched out on the scorched deck of a sailboat, packed between strangers on a ferry—Sydney Harbour was their playground, their glittering refuge. But while they played, far away in Europe, Hitler marched his troops into Poland. Britain declared war, Australia by her side. If it hadn't been for the Second World War, the Maiers may never have stopped travelling. As it was, by the end of 1939, all private travel was stopped. They belonged to Sydney now.

Sydney was the kind of place where you could see a seagull flitting through traffic. Trams trundled down Pitt Street, neon signs towering above—'City Hatters', 'Regent Theatre', 'Royal Arcade'—the letters sat one above the next, ribbons of text threading down the front of every building. Horns honked and news vendors hollered, the underground railway rumbled away. Glasses chinked in bars, while lights blinked on the marquees of picture theatres, one to be found at every turn. But despite the thrill of the city—the sparkling modernity of the brand-new 1940s—in Sydney you were always close to the water. The parks were green and lush, you could smell the sea on the air.

The Union Circulation Company allowed Karl to open a branch in Sydney where he and Alys would continue to sell and distribute subscriptions to the same American publications that they had represented overseas. Karl rented an office in Challis House, a dignified sandstone building on Martin Place in the heart of the city. Alys worked in the office with her husband, assisting wherever she could with the administration of the business. When there was no typing or ordering to do, she would visit nearby businesses to peddle subscriptions. She liked working as a saleswoman. She developed a gift for persuasion, for applying just the right amount of charm to close a sale. She wore a blazer pinched at the waist, twisted her hair into an elegant knot and carried a portfolio under her arm. Men dipped their hats to her as she walked through the streets, weaving her way between swinging briefcases.

She met Paul Haege in his office where she sold him subscriptions to *Newsweek* and *Reader's Digest*. He seemed a little arrogant, a little cavalier, but she was glad to meet another German. They fell into conversation with ease and were able to talk frankly. During her days of travelling from office to office, Alys spouted Karl's opinions with confidence—it was nice to finally meet someone who could reflect those same views back. They spoke of the war, of life in Sydney—of what the future might hold. Paul invited the Maiers to play bridge at his flat in the art-deco Macleay Regis tower at Elizabeth Bay, welcoming them into his circle of Sydney-based Europeans.

Karl and Alys liked Australians, these bold and brash not-quite-Brits. Even with the gloom of war hanging over Sydney, there was always raucous laughter to be found between men at the local pub, a reassuring easiness to the local perspective. While they liked Australians, they weren't accepted as Australians. Of that, they were always aware. In 1901, Edmund Barton's federal government had passed the *Immigration Restriction Act*—also known as the White Australia policy—which made it virtually impossible for non-Europeans to enter the country, using an almost impassable dictation test as its weapon of choice. Prospective non-European immigrants had to write out fifty words in a European language—the catch being that an immigration officer was free to select at random *any* European language. Germans were classed as enemy aliens and existed under constant threat of internment. The system had been kind to the Maiers so far—Alys had been issued a certificate of exemption from the dictation test, Karl avoided being sent off to a camp—but they remained outsiders in every possible way. Meeting other outsiders was like coming up for air.

They befriended Paul Haege and his secretary Margot Adams; Russell Evans, a business associate; Daphne Curtis, their secretary at the Union Circulation Company; and Karl Reschovsky, a prominent tailor. They lunched together and caught newsreels at the cinema. After work, while their Australian colleagues returned to the suburbs, the men would congregate at John Wayne Tailoring, the store where Reschovsky worked in the Strand Arcade. The ornate Victorian arcade glowed in the twilight hour—the stained-glass windows cast colour on Karl's face as he threw back scotch with his friends. At night, the circle flitted between one inner-city flat or another, congregating to play cards and drink, throwing dinner and cocktail parties on the weekends.

It was the first time Alys had been part of a clique. She'd had casual friends at university and during the years of travel with Karl, but not like this—not a real group of her own. The pleasure of belonging bubbled up inside of her, warming her from within like the hot *juk* her mother had served her for breakfast as a child. Margot Adams soon became her first ever *best* friend. The two twenty-four-year-olds spent hour after hour together, doing all the things she'd always imagined best friends do. Drinking coffee and people-watching from the café at Mark Foys department store, recuperating after hours spent ruffling through furs and chiffon. They sent notes between their offices, keeping one another up to date on the events of the working day. On weekends, they spent lazy days in the Botanical Gardens, ignoring the harbour views as they shared their most intimate secrets.

'I'm never enough for Karl,' said Alys, one sunny Saturday, as they strolled along the path by the water at the bottom of the gardens. 'He always has somewhere else to be. It feels as though he'd rather be anywhere else…'

'All men are that way,' said Margot. 'They hate to feel tied down by their wives.'

'I worry,' Alys replied, her imagination drifting away from the picturesque gardens and off to darker places. 'Sometimes I can't help but imagine he spends his evenings with other women.'

'Have you ever asked him?'

'He calls me suspicious. He says my jealousy is stupid.'

Margot never called Alys suspicious or stupid. Instead, she reassured her, hoisting her back up into the sunshine.

'You're a beautiful, intelligent, talented woman. I know that Karl adores you.'

Margot was in love with her employer, Paul Haege. She orbited around him day and night, clinging to the morsels of affection that he cast her way. Alys followed Margot and Paul's push-and-pull romance as though it were a gripping novel. Eventually, when Paul cast Margot aside for good, Alys spent tear-filled days by her friend's side.

The more the pair shared, the more their days were bound together, interwoven by the web of their doubts and delights. Alys thought back to her days at Moscow High, always separate from the girls in her class—she had never known it could be like this. Over time, she began to settle into Sydney and make the city home.

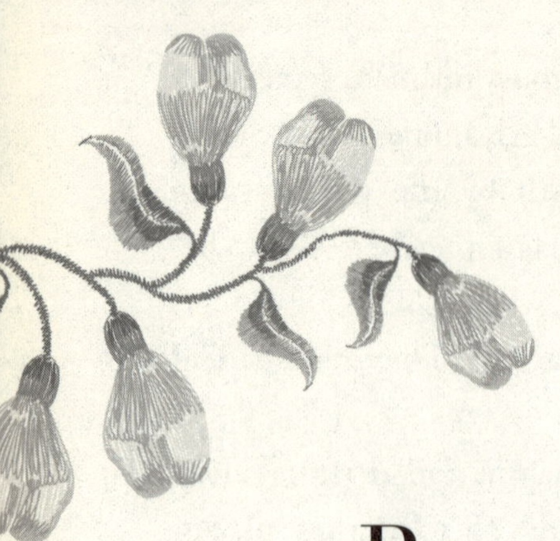

Receptionist

On weekdays in winter, Sydney was cloaked in black. Black suits, black coats, black stockings—hordes of commuters merged together into a single dark mass, swarming through the doors of trains and then outwards up escalators and onto streets. I slipped into the crowd, travelling from one office to the next, working as a temp receptionist. My first job was at a magazine, then at a law firm, then a tech juggernaut—I learnt to adapt my clothes and manner to suit the culture. I sat in stark concrete rooms with nebulous glass lights, wearing pin-sharp stilettos, and in cosy offices the size of a closet, with brown filing cabinets that overflowed with paper. Answering the phones and booking couriers was easy—it was fitting right into the middle of things that was the art to being a receptionist. So I worked to make a place for myself, to improve daily life in each of the businesses I visited.

But that same thought was always there, lingering at the back of my mind: this wasn't what I was supposed to be doing. At least I was paying the bills. At least I could keep my pantry stocked until I figured out what to do next. The temp work kept me busy most days. The rest of my time was spent overhauling the apartment and working on freelance writing and design. I contributed a handful of articles to Flair, but I also started working on illustrations for the site. I painted astrological signs in watercolour, hearts for Valentine's Day.

Working for Flair as a freelancer was a completely different experience from working there as an intern. The change was dramatic and instantaneous. Maja placed significance on the fact that her interns were working for free, she put in real effort to compensate their time with experience, to be grateful and encouraging. For her interns there was room for error, some space for a learning curve. Now that I was a paid employee—however rarely or little I was paid—she was determined to get her money's worth. Horrified at the thought of being ripped off, she was demanding and particular. The process of editing articles seemed to go on indefinitely. We sent emails back and forth for days until I had spent far more time editing a piece than on originally writing it. Sometimes I spent so long working on articles that my hourly rate was reduced to less than a fifth of the minimum wage.

I figured that it was just a learning experience, that I needed to improve. When Maja felt she wasn't getting what she paid for, her wrath was fierce. It was a side of her that I'd seen before, but one that had never been unleashed in my direction. As an intern I listened to her explode in anger, severing relationships with contributors, hanging up the phone and declaring to us all, 'I would cut off my nose to spite my face.' She transformed from raging bull to giggling girlfriend, turning back to us to gossip and laugh it all off. Now I was the one she was turning away from.

When she called to offer me a permanent full-time position, I couldn't have been more shocked. I could hear her excitement burbling down the line. She was eager for me to be part of her team. Perhaps my deficiencies only existed in my mind. She offered me the position of assistant online producer, a significant step up and an opportunity to have a hand in orchestrating connections and content for Flair. I could give up the reception work and give up worrying about how to make ends meet. It was everything I had been working towards, everything that I wanted. Or at least it had been six months earlier.

Interrogation

Alys was home alone in the flat she shared with Karl on Macleay Street, Elizabeth Bay, typing a letter to her parents in China. It was the evening of 1 February 1941, and since war broke out with Japan, her parents had been stranded in China, restricted by the government from returning to the States. Cora and Bob—Idaho-born American citizens—had been sent back to the safety of Moscow in 1937 to be raised by their sister, Marie. It had been a long time since Alys last heard from her parents—via a Red Cross message—but she optimistically wrote to them, hoping for news. Her mind was a million miles away—in the bomb-shattered city of Nanking—when Detective Constable Fraser and Constable Marshall arrived at her door.

As they conducted a search, riffling through the apartment, the policemen kept looking back at Alys. They didn't believe a word she said. What kind of wife couldn't find her husband at nine o'clock in the evening? They asked her about her relationship with Karl—when had they been married? Why had they come to Sydney? Why didn't they have any children? She turned to her experience as a saleswoman and exploited her sparkling charm. She spoke to them as though she had nothing to hide. But the more she spoke, the angrier they grew.

They found Karl's German passport and a postcard he'd received from his brother Hans. They passed the card between them, muttering under their breath. She could see the photograph on the front of the card—the Führer, accepting a bouquet of flowers from a collection of Aryan children who stood up straight, their hands thrust straight in the air. Hans' words were scrawled across the back in German.

Dear Karl,

From this year's Reich-Party Day in Nuremberg where I am on business.

With Heil Hitler,
Yours, Hans

As the hours passed her resolve fell to pieces. She was no longer the charming representative of the Union Circulation Company, no longer Karl's beautiful, witty wife. She wasn't even the little girl from Moscow, Idaho, who trekked across the university campus, carrying her violin. She was smaller than all of those women, smaller than anyone she had ever been before.

When Karl finally strolled through the door his figure was blurred by her tears.

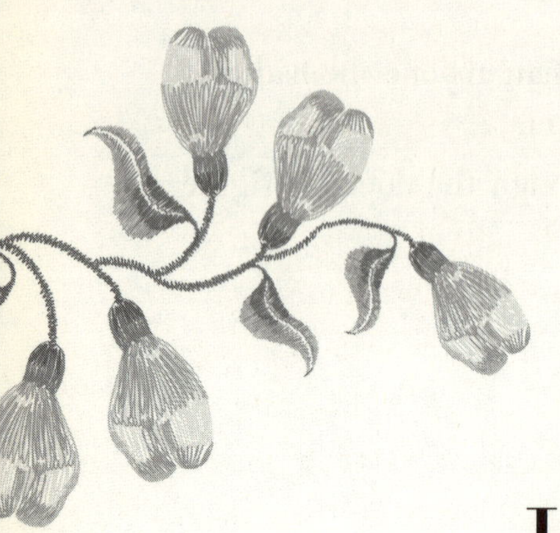

Hers

Whenever Alys' friends asked her how she felt, she lied. She used dramatic words to describe her misery, publicly grieving her husband's imprisonment. She told herself the very same lies because the truth was too scandalous to admit. The truth was, she felt happy.

Karl was interned in February 1941, a year and a half into the war, by which time almost all Germans living in Australia were interned. He was taken first to a camp in Orange, New South Wales, and then transferred down to Tatura in Victoria. The Maiers had always known internment was a threat and there had been plenty of time for Alys to imagine what it would be like. The picture was clear in her mind for months before the day finally came—sleepless nights, weeping in bed—but now that it was here, the reality didn't match that picture. She cycled through the appropriate emotions—fear, sadness, loneliness—but try as she might, she couldn't make them stick. She was alone for the first time in years, but she was not lonely.

Karl handed over much of the daily running of the Union Circulation Company office to a friend, Robert Clark. Decision making and delegating of tasks was left to Alys. She did what work she could, though the business was often stagnant due to the austerity of wartime. Some nights she went to the cinema with Margot. Others, she came home and cooked herself dinner, staying up late to type letters to family and friends.

She began to immerse herself in life around Elizabeth Bay. By day, she ran errands around the winding streets, moving between the bustling stores, gloomy terraces and art-deco apartment buildings. Each time she stopped by the fruit shop she had a chat to Ian McMaster, and she always passed by the pharmacy to say hello to Marea Kelly. The more faces she knew, the more she felt a part of the community. With a pot of tea, she would sit out on her damp, ivy-clad balcony of an evening, looking down over the street below.

As she grew accustomed to the rhythm of local life, she felt herself becoming Australian. She began to belong to the streets as much as they belonged to her. Not since she was sixteen had she stayed in one place for so long, now she was twenty-five. Karl was interned for one month, then two, then three, then more—soon it was over a year. Alys no longer had to worry about where he was and what he was doing. The dinners she prepared tasted better than before—now that she wasn't wondering why he hadn't come home to share them. There was something thrilling about coming home to a flat that was just hers. And the longer Karl was gone, the more her life in Sydney felt like just that—hers. She hated to admit it, but she finally felt free.

She spent her time with the same old set. Having broken off from Paul Haege, Margot had taken up with a Scottish scientist by the name of David Forbes Martyn. David was engaged in top-secret radiography work with Sydney University and the Royal Australian Air Force. He loved plants and animals, the Earth and the atmosphere and the mysteries of outer space. He told Margot and Alys about everything from the life cycle of butterflies to the deterioration of the environment. David was kind and charismatic and falling for Margot. Alys thought watching her friends fall in love was the most marvellous show in the world.

Alys did miss Karl. Not quite the way she'd expected to, but she missed her husband's morning kisses, the gossip they whispered in one another's ears on the tram ride into town. The camp provided internees with paper, twenty-two lines per sheet, two sheets a week. Karl filled his two sheets with details of life in the camp and of his fellow internees. Never a big reader, he asked Alys to send him books and he began to learn Cantonese and study Chinese culture. Alys kept him up to date with the floundering business, sharing life in Sydney and painting a picture of the world beyond the camp fences. Alys' younger sister, Cora, now eighteen years old, wrote him letters in Cantonese to help him practise. In turn, Alys wrote letters to Cora, confiding in her sister. She drew closer to her family, despite the miles between them. Writing about her days allowed her to see the woman she'd become. Wondering about the future could bring on a wave of doubt—but for now, in Elizabeth Bay, she felt a sense of self-assuredness. For now, she'd found her home.

Hunched over the desk in his office, Lieutenant Sandford read all of the internees' mail. Scouring piles of correspondence, he examined every word, searching for clues, for treasonous messages that might be sent in code. He signed off on every letter that was sent to the camp at Tatura—stamping and forwarding them to their recipients, alerting his superiors if anything was amiss. Mrs Maier's letters were better than any of the other wives'. Full of romance and contemplation, they were chronicles of an adventurous past. Sandford looked forward to her bi-weekly correspondence.

> *What do you suppose happened to Mrs Shirtcliffe? To Molly Lee? To Al Overton? I've been wondering today about them, and many others we knew during the last few years. Strange to think that we have so very few friends, yet we've known so many people. Or rather, that when we have known so many people, we have so few friends. And wondering about these people recalls again the days in which we met them—days in Africa and in India, in Burma, in Ceylon, in Malaya, and further back still, in the Philippines and in China. Shanghai—I wonder if we shall ever see it again?*

Over time, he began to detect suspicious patterns in the woman's prose. He copied out the most concerning passages and added his own annotations. Then, as per instructions, he attached the extracts to a memorandum and passed it all up the line.

> *Although the letter is one of the writer's usual clever, chatty epistles, it is noteworthy that in the paragraph quoted she mentions practically a complete list of the countries invaded by Japan. In order to check up on this I would be glad if it could be arranged that the addressee's reply be intercepted and handed to this section in order to find the solution to these remarks. The writer is an extremely clever woman and quite capable of passing information in this way.*

Gutted

I had been living in Shan-Yi's apartment for eighteen months and it was time to sell. The real estate agents insisted that much of the contents needed to be moved out and that the furniture deemed acceptable be rearranged to create an 'open plan' aesthetic. My parents had the storeroom emptied, painted, and turned into a bedroom. I scrambled about compiling all of the paperwork that I wanted to keep—all of the letters and documents that I never found the time to read.

Most of Shan-Yi's possessions were sent to an auction house in Annandale. We took the items that we liked or that we found special—but most had to go. Dad had the various pieces of art appraised, keen to prove that they were painted by the artists that Shan-Yi believed them to be. Some were authenticated, others were very good replicas. The Turners were sent to England for assessment at the Tate, but while many experts said that they *might* be real, no one was willing to sign their name to confirmation. It was more likely that they'd been painted by an apprentice of Turner's, or maybe just a very good copycat. To clear out the books—tens of thousands of books—I put a notice on Facebook, inviting friends to come over and take as much as they could carry for free. We offered the remainder to libraries in various countries, only to discover that nobody wants second-hand books. They were sold in mixed bundles at auction.

Finally there were only my own things and empty space left. It was still beautiful, but in a different way—just the curves of the walls and expanses of floorboards. The redundant spaces would surely be gutted—powder room, maid's bedroom, dressing room—to create more functional spaces. The kitchen and bathrooms would have to be completely stripped—the wobbly old oven would be ripped from the kitchen wall.

I moved into a shoebox basement flat in Darlinghurst with rising damp and tiny windows set at street level—but a space that was truly my own. The rent was beyond my budget but I'd been living in an alternate reality, so my expectations were skewed. I stuck pictures on the walls and hung fabric from the ceiling, cut up plastic flowers from the two-dollar shop and threaded them into garlands.

On my final day in Shan-Yi's apartment, I wandered from room to room, taking photos, just as I had when I first moved in. This time I was locking it into my memory. I sat on the balcony, stretched out in the breeze and gazed out over the stalwart harbour, immense and blustery. The great cool blue that I could never quite be part of. It was the last time I would ever sit there.

The apartment meant a lot to me because Shan-Yi meant a lot to me, but also because I loved the place in itself. It was part of my childhood and part of my story. It was somewhere I found beautiful and treasured for that fact. I expected it to be harder to leave—I thought I would cry, but I didn't. It wasn't her place anymore; without her things I couldn't feel her there in the same way that I used to. Shan-Yi's ashes were scattered across the garden—she was long gone. But we weren't finished yet.

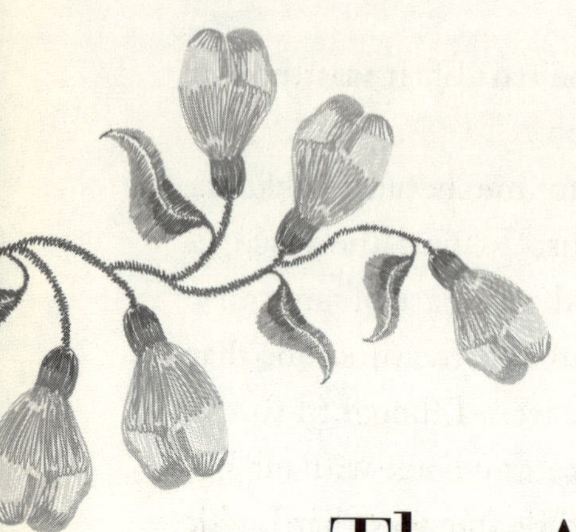

The American

The clock tower of Sydney's General Post Office was dismantled stone by stone. In early 1942, authorities were worried the neoclassical tower might serve as a target for Japanese aircraft, loaded with explosives. Across the road, from the window of her office at Challis House, Alys watched as giant pieces of sandstone were lowered to the ground, traffic forced to a halt. As wartime was thrust upon Sydney, people made adjustments. Food and clothing were rationed, people wept at newsstands, morale-boosting posters plastered the walls. But in many ways, Alys was surprised by how much life carried on as always.

American troops flooded the city, but they rarely crossed Alys' path. Down at the Trocadero nightclub on George Street, Yankee sailors danced with home-grown Aussie girls, swinging to the big-band beat of 'Chattanooga Choo Choo'. But the Trocadero was a whites-only venue and Alys couldn't have gone if she'd wanted to. It didn't matter—she was too caught up with her friends, with late-night digestifs and cigarettes in the bohemian apartments of Potts Point. There, the cafés were Parisian, and the delicatessens sold all the food that Europeans loved from home.

She made her usual commute home from the office to Elizabeth Bay by tram. Riding the tram through traffic on Pitt Street, if you were quick enough you could lean out the window and buy fruit from street-side barrows. Alys made an art of it, correct change in hand, when the tram paused, she'd reach out at just the right second to buy a banana.

Sitting next to her on the tram when she made the purchase one day, American GI Charlie Jones burst out laughing, 'That's the niftiest trick I've ever seen.'

For the next week, they were inseparable. Alys showed Charlie the sights of Sydney, the little harbour beaches that hardly anybody knew; they had lunch at the Australia Hotel and saw *Ringside Maisie* at the State Theatre. The first time he kissed her, she pulled away, but her objections were just for show. She was doing the wrong thing, but it couldn't be wrong to feel so happy.

Charlie was a ball of energy, like a puppy clawing at her side. He overwhelmed her with compliments, the type of sentimental words that Karl would have called 'soft'. His eyes were full of childlike innocence and widened as she spoke. He was five years older than her, but it felt the other way around. He had never seen anything of the world beyond his corn-fed American hometown before the war. Everything she said and did was new. His lilting accent reminded her of home—the pine trees and prairies of Idaho—and if she closed her eyes, she could have been back on Main Street, Moscow, tramping through the snow. Charlie spoke of the children they'd have together; the life they would share in the States. She chose not to think about Karl, instead focusing her attention on the handsome man who offered so many of the things she wanted and had never been able to reach.

Alys went down to the Garden Island naval base at Woolloomooloo to wave goodbye the day that Charlie was due to ship out. She hurried past the dense rows of terraces, wearing their lace dresses and standing tall. She saw him before she reached the dock. There he was, standing beside his vessel, a blonde wrapped tightly in his arms. For a few seconds Alys stood and watched the couple kiss—watched as his fingers grazed her cheek.

Then she turned for home.

Assistant Online Producer

For my first week of full-time work at Flair, I had a cough. It was incessant and deep, the kind that makes you feel as though you've just done a hundred sit-ups. I was a disgusting, spluttering mess, but I was determined not to call in sick—I wanted to prove that I was not a flake, that I was committed to the job. I wanted to prove that I would show up no matter what; but the coughing would not stop.

'That's incredibly annoying,' Maja snapped soon after I arrived. 'Go home. You're doing a grown-up job now; you need to be considerate.'

I drove home in tears, my cheeks burning.

I returned to the office the following week, loaded up on codeine and cough drops, determined to start over. But even on my second attempt, the new role started out shakily. The truth was, I wasn't quite sure what an 'assistant online producer' was. The duties outlined in my contract were much the same as the work I had been doing for the last year as an intern and then as a freelancer. But there was something different in the way that Holly and Maja spoke to me. There was an unspoken shift that had to be learnt. I asked questions—dozens of questions—but there was never time for training or explanation, so I tried my best to learn on the job.

The first event I attended in my new role was a breakfast to promote the launch of a new anti-ageing cream. There was a nutritionist present to speak about the benefits of combining a healthy diet with the best skincare products. I asked all the appropriate questions to write an article about the product and took a handful of photos for Instagram, but when I returned to the office, Maja was furious that I hadn't secured a follow-up interview with the nutritionist. That kind of content would be perfect for our wellbeing section.

'What was the point of sending you?' she demanded. 'What did we get out of the two hours that you were away from the office?'

I felt like a moron. Of course I should have taken the opportunity to gain valuable expert content for Flair. That was what producers did. But at all the events I attended as an intern I'd just smiled on behalf of the team, taking photos and returning with products to be featured in listicles and galleries. I'd always received a big thumbs-up.

There were other times when I made thoughtless mistakes and really should have known better. I was frustrated with myself, but I was also frustrated with Maja. I could see my mistakes and I could see the room for improvement. What I couldn't understand was why she had to be so harsh—why she resorted to snapping and yelling when reasoned feedback would have served just as well. I wanted to tell her to calm down. I guessed being a ball-buster was what made her the editor-in-chief of her very own publication in the first place. She could be irrational at times, but it was expecting the best that kept her at the top of her game. I had a lot to learn from my boss, I just needed to lift *my* game.

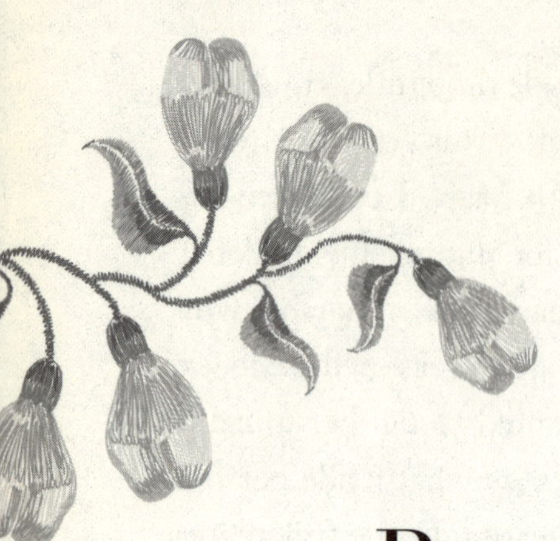

Repentance

For a limited time, Alys was able to disappear into the dream of life with Charlie. But now she was wide awake. She was seventeen when she first met Karl. Now twenty-six, they'd been married almost ten years. Karl was the man who chose her, the one who had been by her side through it all. And he was waiting at the camp, relying on her letters as his only source of reprieve. What she had shared with Charlie was superficial, empty. The love she shared with Karl was built for a lifetime.

She had been to visit Karl at the camp in Tatura twice before, counting every minute of the twelve-hour train ride, longing to see him. But this time, the journey felt like minutes. She'd decided to tell Karl about Charlie and her mind was racing, making and unmaking the decision in a never-ending cycle of conviction and doubt. She reminded herself that this was the only way to repent.

When she told Karl what she had done, he grabbed both of her wrists and squeezed them so tightly that she worried he might sever her circulation. He drew his face towards her, looking her straight in the eye.

'You're telling me the truth?'

'Yes.'

'And it was just this one man?'

'Yes, just Charlie.'

'Charlie!' he spat the word like it was poison. 'That was his name? Don't you ever say it again.'

He pulled her closer towards him. She wasn't sure if he was going to kiss her or thrust her backwards onto the ground. He was holding her wrists so tight that she was certain he could send her flying. But then his gaze softened. 'Okay.'

She had imagined hours of yelling, imagined returning to Sydney, her face blotchy and swollen from tears. But Karl released her wrists and kissed her on the forehead.

'I know you won't do this again,' he said, as though he were speaking to himself as much as to her. 'I love you. You're the only thing keeping me sane in here, the only thing I want to escape for.'

Her whole body melted in relief, falling in to his chest.

'Our marriage is the one thing that matters,' he said. 'We only have each other.'

While he searched her eyes, she felt as though she was seventeen all over again. He held her close, stroking her back, the smell of him seeping through her. Everything was going to be okay.

When the time came to leave the internment camp,

she didn't want to go. She kissed her husband goodbye, surrounded by the brown Victorian bushland—she could hear the whipbirds calling. A male and a female, singing their duet, closing with that signature crack. She ignored Karl's inmates, watching on from beyond the chicken-wire fence—her eyes followed his figure as he turned and walked away. She had no idea it was the last time they would hold each other close.

The Monkey

I jumped every time the doorbell rang. And the doorbell rang a lot. There are many reasons for a woman to leap from her seat when a courier arrives with beauty products, but fear isn't usually one of them.

I was never a skittish person, but you wouldn't have believed it if you'd seen me around the Flair office, spinning and yelping at the slightest noise. I had become timid and highly strung, a mouse in the lion's den. But I *wasn't* a mouse, I wasn't a quitter. I knew that I could handle this job, if I could only overcome the fact that the very sound of Maja's voice made me break into a sweat.

I never knew what was going to set her off. It was always when I thought I was doing well that she would grow suddenly angry—when I thought I had missed the mark that she showered me in praise. She loved me and loathed me in an irregular pattern—I never knew which was coming next.

When writing for someone like Maja, you need to learn to write in their voice. Bubbly but informed, fun but sophisticated—there was a specific language to be used in a Flair article. My writing hadn't changed since I was an intern, but in my new role Maja seemed to hate everything that I wrote. Perhaps it was that she was paying closer and closer attention—she parsed through my pieces carefully, finding error with every word. Her disappointment extended beyond my writing. She hated my Instagram posts, hated the photographs I took. My instincts were all wrong.

The truth was, I couldn't anticipate her ever-changing instincts, couldn't figure out how to think the way she would. Her reflexes were the opposite of mine—except for the times when they weren't. Since she loved everything that Holly produced, I knew it was *possible* to please her, possible to succeed.

I was hitting against the limits of my imagination. In that regard, my writing actually *was* getting worse. I couldn't think of new ways to get excited about beauty products, I couldn't think of new words to describe the perfect brow. The truth crept in between my words—I was telling stories that I wouldn't want to hear, selling women products and treatments that I didn't really think they needed. The confusion seeped into my writing. Maja was right, my words didn't dazzle.

'These captions are all completely boring!' she would say. 'Come up with a different perspective. This isn't just monkey see, monkey do!'

That was her favourite phrase. Monkey see, monkey do. And it always seemed to apply to me. I was trying to be creative—to find words that popped off the page—but all she could see was the same old fluff, the filler that characterised the rest of the internet. Exactly what Flair wasn't supposed to be. I was failing at the things that I thought I did best. I was failing as a writer, failing at finding a voice. When I worked on administrative tasks or made phone calls, Maja said, '*This* is what you should do. *This* is what you do well.' It was just as the careers advisor told me—I should be working in office administration.

If I couldn't improve my writing, I figured I would focus on the work that Maja *did* appreciate. I studied Google analytics and researched SEO, I worked through the site changing headlines and URLs to improve our readership. We were always chasing clicks, trying to write the holy grail—a viral post—so I diverted my efforts towards achieving that goal. But the clicks led us off in different directions, steering us away from our original course. Sometimes I wasn't sure where we were headed or who our target audience was. Our horoscopes section was the most popular, so we boosted horoscopes, promoting them on Instagram. Suddenly we were an astrology publication. Celebrity gossip did well as did television recaps—so we wrote about shows that we didn't always watch. We leapt from place to place, chasing clicks, raising our ratings but looking less and less like the publication that we were supposed to be.

The more uncertain I felt about who we were and where we were headed, the more my work suffered. But I didn't want to quit. If I was a true writer I could write anything for anyone. If I was a hard worker I could make this happen. Besides, if I gave up on Flair after just a few months in a full-time role, I could kiss a career in online publishing goodbye. I worked to impress the woman who regretted giving me a job.

But the doorbell kept ringing and I kept jumping.

Woodford

Karl decided Alys would be better off out of the city, away from the wharves of Woolloomooloo. He arranged for her to move in with Mrs Edna Berger and Mrs Clara Hoffman, the wives of two of his fellow internees. The pair were living in a cottage in the tiny village of Woodford in the Blue Mountains and Karl liked the idea of Alys safely tucked away with nothing but the kookaburras and crisp morning dew to attract her wandering eye. Edna and Clara worked as nurses at Yama, a convalescent home for tuberculosis patients. At Karl's request, Alys would be joining their efforts.

As she travelled north on the train out of Sydney, her nameless German shepherd companion licked her face. Shan-Yi was bringing the dog because Clara had written to her saying: 'It's not safe for three women to live on their own, we need a guard dog to keep watch.'

Alys talked to the animal, ruffling his shaggy neck. She lifted him up to look out the window, pointing out the beaten tracks hidden among the eucalyptus trees. She liked the trees and wildflowers, the hairpin banksias with their copper-coloured spires. But she was unimpressed with the mountains, or at least unimpressed by their size. The mountains of Washington state put these self-important hills to shame.

For all her years of fast-paced typing, Alys had never really done any manual labour. She imagined herself in an apron and a nurse's cap—'the lady with the lamp' flitting from bedside to bedside, tending to wounded soldiers. Of course, she wouldn't actually be working with soldiers and, having no experience to speak of, she was unlikely to be given any serious duties. Still, she was eager to contribute. As much as she loved Margot and their circle of friends in Sydney's Eastern Suburbs, the many months of frolicking about during wartime had left her with a desire to do something serious.

She had never been so busy as she was during her first weeks in Woodford. The three women worked long days at Yama, then returned home to hour after hour of cleaning. The house they rented was old and decrepit and they spent days dusting and polishing, emptying the rooms of all the junk previous tenants had abandoned, not to mention beating the bush out of the garden, breaking off branches and clipping at weeds. Lying in bed, legs aching at the end of another day, Alys listened to the possums scampering over the corrugated-iron roof. When it rained it sounded like great sheets of water, rather than drops, blanketing the little home. The thunder and lightning were deafening.

She held her pillow over her ears, desperate to get a good night's sleep.

On top of her duties at the convalescent home, she continued to work for the Union Circulation Company. She wrote letters to subscribers all over the country, apologising for late deliveries and unfulfilled orders. Their associate, Robert Clark, visited her on weekends with updates from the office. The business wasn't doing well: war meant paper shortages, and a number of the magazines they represented weren't being produced at all.

Alys was too busy working to notice the eyes that followed her, peering through shelves in the grocery store, spying out of the lace-curtained windows of houses she passed. She was too hurried to stop and listen to the footsteps behind her, too preoccupied to wonder about the thoughts of nameless strangers on the street. She didn't hear the whispers, didn't see the bowed heads—didn't notice those who noticed her.

She was playing the diligent maid, replacing bed clothes at Yama, when a stranger approached the post box just a short way down the street. With a nod of his head, the gentleman slid his envelope through the slot. His chest puffed out as he receded down the street, his civic duty done. He was a good Australian citizen, a loyal subject of the Queen's Commonwealth.

The Officer-in-Charge Police Dept. Sydney

Dear Sir,

I can give you no definite statements on the following,

but feel it is my duty to call your attention to the matter as I know it.

Naturally being a resident in this town I prefer to remain anonymous.

At 'Yama' Convalescent Home in Woodford, there is a Chinese woman boarding. Whether she is Chinese or not, I'm not qualified to judge—but rumour here has it that her husband is an interned German. If this is so, it does not seem to fit in with the fact that a loyal Chinese would be boarding, or working, for people who are reputed to be the friends of her interned husband and of German origin.

All I know is that she is a very attractive oriental, who wears expensive clothes, and seems to have quite a bit of time on her hands.

When she first arrived she had an Alsatian bitch with her. This dog was recently sent away, and the story circulated that it had bitten a man and was being sent to the RSPCA. The guard on the station was stated as not being able to get near the dog to put a ticket on its collar, and that its owner had previously attached an envelope to its collar.

There is another peculiar feature to the case. About every few weeks on a Sunday the Chinese woman goes to the station and meets with a man (tall and very fair) who always carries an attaché case, and seems to return to town on the same day.

Another strange feature is that when on the train coming to Woodford, she was stated as saying 'that she was ready for work.'

I do not know whether this information will be of

interest to you, but I do know that the following facts do not fit in very well.

1. 'Yama' is a tuberculosis convalescent home and in such places healthy boarders are not usually taken (even if friends of the family).

2. If a Chinese, it seems strange she should take refuge with a family reputed to be of German descent.

3. If working as a maid, her expensive attire and amount of leisure time is out of keeping.

4. She speaks perfect English and has apparently been very well educated.

5. Maids are not usually allowed to bring their pet animal with them to their prospective position.

I hope I am not wasting your valuable time, but feel as there are quite a lot of things which pass along this road that would interest many, I felt it my duty to inform you, and leave it to your Department to decide whether it is worth an investigation.

Yours truly,
P.

The Violin

Shan-Yi's photographs hung on the walls of my new Darlinghurst apartment. Her records and diaries stood on the shelves along with the piles of untouched paperwork and thirty-four kilograms of her correspondence, I weighed it to quantify the volume of paper to friends and family. A pair of her guardian lions stood by the door, the male with his paw resting on a ball, the female with a cub underfoot. I called the lions Shan-Yi and Andrew, except Shan-Yi was the male with the whole world at her feet.

I kept her beautiful Italian violin, made in the late eighteenth century, cradled in its leather case lined with purple velvet. I'd found it soon after I moved into her apartment, wedged against a door, being used as a doorstop. If anything I kept was an extension of her, I figured the violin was it. I wondered when she stopped playing. She had risked everything to be a violinist, but it seemed she was swept off course and never found her way back to the very idea that got her started. It made me anxious to think that she'd been side-tracked by life. I had no idea if she could have been the next Kreisler, but it felt like that *should* have been the case. My father certainly couldn't remember her ever playing.

Shan-Yi was never taught to throw caution to the wind, to do everything it took in pursuit of her dreams. 'Believe in yourself', 'you can be anything', 'success never comes to those who quit'—these stock motivational slogans were as much a part of my education as addition and the alphabet. I was a child of the nineties, a product of Girl Power, a grade-A student in the technicolour classroom of Disney. I followed my dreams as a matter of course. The reality that raw talent—and more importantly, blind luck—had a role to play in success seemed utterly unfair. But I couldn't hide from the fact that I'd been writing and drawing and working for years and I hadn't made it anywhere. Maybe she *could* have been the next Kreisler if life had taken a different course. Maybe she was just unlucky.

However, I know she considered herself *lucky*. She told us so, right up until the end when her feet were covered in bedsores and it hurt to move at all. She believed that her life was full of extraordinary luck. Not the kind of luck that people mention in gratitude, but real, logic-defying, larger-than-life luck. The kind that prevents you from tripping on a loose step, even when gravity insists that you should. She couldn't comprehend the hand she'd been dealt. But it seemed she never achieved the dream that put fire in her belly in the first place. Her beautiful violin had gathered dust for decades and disappeared into the cluttered apartment.

The thought of leaving Flair had been on my mind since I started full-time. The job never felt right and I never seemed to fit. It was one thing to duck in and out of that world a few days a week—but living in it every day was exhausting. It was breaking me down; I was losing touch with who I was again.

Nevertheless, I didn't want to give up. I wasn't a quitter. I had been given luxuries and opportunities that Shan-Yi never had; I could make my dreams come true in ways that she never could. She started out with eleven dollars, riding a lonely bus through Washington's Wenatchee National Forest. I started out with every advantage in the world. Except working at Flair was never really my dream. My dreams of writing a novel were gathering dust, just like her violin.

I wanted to reach into her violin and find whatever it was in her that I couldn't find in me. I wanted her to teach me how to feel happy, no matter the path life takes.

Free

For all the letters Alys typed and the invoices she sent, she never had custody of the key to the post box. The keys belonged to Karl, along with the bank accounts, the business files, their identification cards, and the car. When Karl was interned, he asked that she pass these crucial items onto Robert. That was just the way Karl was—always in charge. It never occurred to her that he *needed* to keep the keys to himself; she never suspected there were secrets in the mail.

When business at the Union Circulation Company took another dive, Karl conceded that the situation was unsustainable and he handed over the business to his wife, who promptly returned to Sydney from Woodford. For the first time ever, the company was fully in her hands. And the keys to the post box were hers. After several months in Woodford, she had a newfound sense of industriousness—the feeling of being a contributor. But much as the manual work provided her with a sense of achievement, she knew she would be better at running the office than being a maid.

Soon after her return from the Blue Mountains, she found a letter addressed to Karl in the company post box from an acquaintance by the name of Miss May Beeton, a woman who had assisted around the office when the Maiers first moved to Sydney. The language in the letter was coquettish, overly familiar—but it wasn't exactly damning. Alys told herself May was just being friendly, just trying to stay in touch.

Shortly after that, a second letter came from Irene, Alys' girlfriend from back in Johannesburg. Alys recognised the handwriting on the envelope and tore it open, excited to receive news from South Africa. But the letter had not been written with Alys in mind. She was two pages in before her own name made an appearance.

> *Remember the night the Dutchman and Alys disappeared into the kitchen? Were they fixing cherry brandy? I don't recall. Whatever the reason, you and I were left alone. Your kisses were sweet and swift, nobody would even know your lips had been on mine … though I could feel them there for the rest of the night …*

She was too shocked to cry.

She read the letter over and over until the words became fractured from their meaning, just letters on a sheet of paper, spinning round and round. Imre filled page after page with scenes that Alys had never witnessed, her descriptions explicit. Intimate encounters that weren't just carnal, but full of passion and feeling.

For days after reading Irene's letter, she ransacked the flat, tearing through the pockets of Karl's jackets, leafing through all of his books. In the lining of his trunk she found photographs of a woman, lazing nude in the first-class cabin of the liner aboard which Alys had met Karl at Dar-es-Salaam. She thought of all the times Karl had travelled alone, all of the ships that he boarded without her. She lay awake at night, her imagination full of steam liners, of hotel rooms in foreign cities, of nights they invited women into their Sydney home. No memory was safe from suspicion; no special moment unsoured.

The final blow wasn't delivered by a letter, but from the mouth of a friend. Bernice Sanders, had the full account—her husband was a close friend of Karl's. It seemed the truth was well known down in the smoky comfort of John Wayne Tailoring, where Karl had spoken of his conquests not once, but many times. Bernice told Alys everything in vivid detail. There were more women than she had ever imagined, even in her most fretful nights of worry and doubt. Secretaries from neighbouring offices in Challis House, women overseas, women in Sydney who had been her friends. It was laughable, really, just how many there were. Karl always called her suspicious, but she was never suspicious enough. For all the times she doubted herself, all the times she felt like a mad woman, she had been right from the start.

She became desensitised to the image of her husband making love to other women. But as the weeks went by, that wasn't what haunted her dreams. Everybody—apart from Margot—seemed to have known. She felt betrayed by this community of strangers she thought were her friends. Her husband had played her for a fool and she was mortified and ashamed. How could she trust anyone at all, when almost everyone she knew fed her such bald lies?

Her most bitter memory was the thought of the trip she made down to Tatura, to confess her own infidelity. She had offered herself up in repentance to Karl and tearfully admitted to an affair that had been little more than flirtation. Karl's hypocrisy, painting her as the scarlet woman, chastising her and playing the moral superior: the last ten years of her life were a lie.

It was a blessing, then, that Margot hadn't known. She was grateful for that, to have one person left to trust. And so it was in Margot that she confided the truth.

'Karl and I will never be together again.'

Alys' travel privileges were revoked after she failed to notify the authorities of her move to the Blue Mountains. Unable to leave the state and visit Tatura, there were no means by which she could speak to her husband in person, at least not until the war ended. Karl had been interned for two years and despite initial optimism, news from abroad suggested the conflict would drag on. As angry as she was, as ferociously as she railed against him in private, she would not abandon him while he was still a prisoner. She would wait until he was released before she told him that he had no wife to come home to.

Flying

I was sitting in a chartered jet full of fashion writers, pinching myself. We marched through the airport like an army of high-heeled soldiers, dressed in a uniform of black and white—sunglasses on heads, overnight cases in tow. Now, we were cruising through the air towards Melbourne for the launch of the first H&M store in Australia.

Even among the most disenchanted of bloggers and influencers there was a sense of excitement. The retail juggernaut had a budget to blow and we were expecting something beyond the average sparkle of a launch. The regular Qantas headrest covers were replaced by H&M branding, as though there was any chance that we might forget why we were there. We would all stay the night at the Crown Hotel in Southbank—as for the launch party itself, the festivities were a closely guarded secret.

I felt light and easy, excited about the overnight adventure.

Perhaps it was the distance from the Flair office but I felt better about my job than I had done in months. If I could just relax for a second, maybe I could create better content. My assignment was to cover the event on Instagram, post an article and a gallery.

A red carpet was rolled out onto Bourke Street Mall and TV personalities, musicians, and models were being photographed on their way into the store. The vast Victorian building centred around a three-storey atrium. The columns were painted white to match the marble floors, the space was clean and fresh, mannequins sat on swings that hung from the ceilings high above. Down below, guests were unleased on the fashion, eating canapés and drinking cocktails while we shopped. I bought a dress for a friend's upcoming wedding. As the night carried on, LA-born band-of-the-moment Haim took to the DJ booth, spinning Spice Girls and Beyoncé songs while shoppers danced in the middle of the store.

I filmed an Instagram video throughout the night, cutting shots together as I moved through the store. I wanted to put our readers inside the launch, taking them down the red carpet and all the way up to the highest floor, giving them a glimpse of the entire event. I was happy with the final product. I left before it got too late, catching a cab back to the hotel to put together coverage of the event. Sitting in my suite writing, I enjoyed recounting an event that I had experienced first-hand, rather than just recycling content. It was the kind of writing that I understood, the kind of writer that I wanted to be. I looked down over Melbourne, the blaze of city lights trickling down into the river. I felt a buzz as I tapped away on my laptop, surrounded by the sleek hotel room. It was as though I was an entirely different person; somebody professional and important who knew what she was doing.

At the airport the following morning, we were all slouched over laptops and phones, using the free Wi-Fi to get work done before flying. The excitement of the previous day had evaporated, replaced by anxiety over meetings missed and desk-time lost. I received an email from Maja and opened it with my usual trepidation—holding my breath and wishing that she could have waited until I was safely on board and off the grid. But my fear was for nought—she loved my coverage of the event. After trawling through every other publication's Instagram she decided that my video was her favourite of the night. She was thrilled with my article and photo gallery, pleased with the captions that I'd written.

There was a moment of delight, and then just relief. As I boarded the plane and fell into my seat I breathed easier than I had in months. I knew that I was flying towards congratulations. But even in my moment of triumph, as the plane neared Sydney, relief gave way to dread. If I relaxed and focused and got to work, I *could* do this job. I *could* please Maja. I just didn't want to. I was out of my depth from the moment I walked into the permanent role. Not because I wasn't capable of learning, but because I didn't belong there. If I stayed I would improve—I would get there eventually—but I'd never be able to compete with women who lived and breathed beauty and lifestyle. I couldn't fake their passion and dedication. Why was I putting all my time and energy into squeezing myself into a frame that didn't fit? What was I trying to prove?

*

I survived my resignation, but not without a bundle of tissues in hand. Sitting beside me on the silver sofa, Maja knew what was coming before the words were out of my mouth. She was kind and reassuring and told me I'd made the right decision. She knew it as well as I did—Flair wasn't the place for me.

The Hungarian

Of the many strangers she rode the elevator with at Challis House, he was the most interesting—the man with the monogrammed leather suitcase: A.G.B. He always said 'Good day' when he stepped into the wrought iron cage, his voice as deep as a double bass with a husky Eastern European accent. He struck Alys as shy, often averting his gaze as soon as the greeting was through. Perhaps his voice was so deep because he was trying to bury his words within him, hiding them away. The operator swung the lever, and up or down they'd go, riding the rest of the way in silence.

They rode the elevator together hundreds of times before they were finally introduced by a mutual friend.

'Mrs Maier, surely you *must* know Andrew Balogh!'

After that, they always chatted in the elevator, the operator bearing witness to their fledgling friendship. She learnt that he ran his own trading company, importing jewellery and curios. He spoke in broken English, putting sentences together upside down, pronouncing 'thank you' as 'tank you', and 'you're welcome' as 'you're velcome'. She teased him for his bad grammar and thought he sounded like the villain from a Hollywood film—something she had never thought about her German husband, who had turned out to be villainous. She knew that he would ask her to lunch for weeks before he finally mustered up the courage to do so. With a laugh she said 'yes'.

Half the time they could barely understand each other, but she felt certain that he knew who she was. Andrew was Jewish–Hungarian and had escaped Europe in 1939 with his sister on one of the last ships to depart unchecked by encroaching Nazi rule. His sister disembarked in British Palestine, while he continued on to Australia with assistance from the Catholic Archbishop of Sydney, whom he had befriended during a visit to Budapest. He was granted refugee status. The life he and his sister left behind was one riddled with fear. But he escaped. He got out lucky. Many of his friends and family were unaccounted for while his mother and another sister had been captured and killed.

As Andrew drew her into his confidence, his dark-brown eyes shining with tears, she felt filthy—as though she had dirt trapped underneath her fingernails, dirt that would be there forever. She couldn't forget how she'd allowed Karl's politics to creep into her life. The times she hadn't thought to question his unwavering patriotism, his allegiance to a nation committing atrocities to which he turned a blind eye.

Andrew was in the middle of a bitter divorce and had a

nine-year-old son, Albin, who lived with him full time. At thirty-six, Andrew was ten years older than Alys, but they spoke as equals. They both had lives that they wished to leave behind, heartaches and loss that they preferred to put in the past. They were ready to start again.

In the final months of 1943, Alys spent time with Andrew and Albin at their lavish, family-sized apartment in Bellevue Hill. At Christmas they hung ornaments together and decorated the windows with golden lights Andrew had imported from Europe. They were the only family on the block to display twinkling globes. One night, officers arrived at the door and demanded the lights be taken down. Andrew and Alys were bewildered as the policemen confiscated their decorations—but the hostility of strangers couldn't dampen their festive spirit.

Andrew rented a flat for Alys in a grand Edwardian building called the Danmark in Point Piper—the ritziest neighbourhood in Sydney's Eastern Suburbs. She kept the flat she shared with Karl and made regular trips back there to collect letters from her husband, but in truth she lived at the Danmark, close to Andrew and Albin.

Most mornings, Andrew picked her up for work and drove her to the city in his sleek Pontiac, while most evenings were spent together on her sofa in comfortable silence, her head resting on his shoulder. When the time came for Andrew to go home to his son, she would stay up late, typing letters to Karl and to her family abroad. She couldn't have gone to sleep if she'd tried—her heart kept a racing beat. The more she got to know Andrew, the more she felt herself, as though she were finally growing closer to the woman she truly was. That woman certainly wasn't 'Alys', the name Karl had chosen for her. She considered going back to being 'Alice', but that name was just invented at an immigration office in Seattle. 'Shan-Yi' was the name she was given at birth. She concocted the spelling herself, but the sound was right. She couldn't be her own woman without using her own name. She would be Shan-Yi from now on.

A Chinese Girl

Shan-Yi's attention was centred on Andrew, but sometimes she sensed others' attention on her. Whether walking along the shady crescents of Point Piper, wading in the harbour at Rose Bay, meeting friends, or coming home from the grocery store, she sometimes felt she was being watched. After Andrew went home to Albin each night, she stayed up late typing her letters. But as the months passed she grew frightened by the solitude, the neighbourhood was dark and there were strange cars parked in her street.

In August of 1944, not far from Shan-Yi's apartment, an anonymous letter arrived at the Sydney Police Station, stamped from the Point Piper post office.

Dear Sir,

For about a year, a Chinese girl lives at the house

Danmark, Wolseley Road, Point Piper. I cannot figure out what she is up to. She is picked up by a green car at nine am and brought back by the same at five pm. Before entering or leaving the house she is always looking around carefully, probably afraid of being watched. I believe she is in a kind of drug business, but lately at night time I can hear a tapping noise like signals from her flat.

Her cigarette I picked up was a German one …

Free Fall

Done with the world of facials and flower arrangements, I returned to sorting paperclips from bulldog clips and keeping files in alphabetical order as a temp receptionist. There were times when the job was frantic—but many hours when my mind was free to wander. I spent hours roaming the internet, reading short stories and newspaper articles, delving into the *Vanity Fair* online crime archive. I became a couch detective, solving my own mysteries on social media. When I received a text from Tom for the first time in a year I wondered why he was contacting me. His girlfriend Jessica posted a picture of her graduation from law school—Tom wasn't there. Their relationship status was no longer public. I asked a friend and she confirmed that they'd broken up.

I always felt things before I thought them, by the time my thoughts caught up with my heart, it was too late. I hadn't thought about Tom for so long, but my body was charged with electricity for days after I found out that he and Jessica had broken up—I felt exhilarated before I could figure out why. It was autumn again, the world kept spinning, and I was spinning with it. But falling in love made it feel okay that I wasn't sure where I was going. Tom and I were both caught in limbo—he had been offered a PhD candidacy at Yale and was waiting for August to start a new life in America. My life as a temp was structureless and strange. We were both on hold, searching for solid ground, so we filled our days with each other.

As autumn turned to winter we behaved more and more like a couple. But even so, that title wasn't ours. We might share the intimacy, the time and co-dependency of a relationship, but Tom made it clear the label of 'girlfriend' wasn't on offer. He was determined not to hurt Jessica or turn our friendship group upside down. Besides, his departure loomed, making a separation inevitable. I understood the logic, but I couldn't help but see danger. I looked back over the recent years of my life and saw depression chasing after me. I didn't want to have my heart broken again so I pushed away, broke free from his grasp.

'I need space. I'm falling for you. We can't be together *all* of the time.'

It didn't work. A couple of days' silence, and then he would be back again. I tried to break away, but we played out the same pattern each time. Sometimes I thought that he couldn't resist his feelings, at times I even indulged in the idea that he *couldn't* stay away. Other times I thought that he simply didn't believe me when I told him how I felt. I worried that he was using me. I worried that I was a place holder, filling up the space left behind by Jessica. But if there was anybody in the world who I could trust it was Tom. He'd watched me piece myself together after my last breakup, he had a front-row seat for my battle with depression. He was the only person who was familiar with all of my deepest darkest parts. Even back in high school, he was the one who lifted me up when I staggered and fell.

If anyone understood the game we were playing it was Tom. He wouldn't risk our friendship, he wouldn't risk hurting Jessica—not if it wasn't worth it, not if he could help it. That wasn't the man that he was. So worry as I might, my heart filled with the truth that he cared. All the trouble would be worth it in the end.

The closer we drew to his departure the closer we drew together. The night before my twenty-sixth birthday, a month before he was due to leave, we finally had sex. I expected it to mean something—I expected there to be fireworks. But if anything, it just felt inevitable. It was just another step forward—a brief tussle and a handful of flesh. Afterwards we lay back in bed the same people that we had always been. We already knew everything that there was to know about each other, there was little left to see. We were already so deep into one another's worlds that we couldn't get any closer.

By the time he left for Yale, I was in love with him. I imagined us living a life together. I wanted to go to America with him, I wanted to start adulthood over—this time with my best friend by my side.

Intelligence

Detective Sergeant 3rd Class Hargrave of the Security Service sat in his patrol car amid the shadows of Wolseley Road, Point Piper. The street was quiet. Alys Maier and Andrew Balogh had entered the Danmark building an hour earlier and Hargrave didn't expect them to come out any time soon. He'd been watching them for weeks and knew their routines.

He leafed through the file by torchlight, searching for some new clue hidden among the well-worn records. Instead, he found the same words that he had already read a thousand times.

Paul HAEGE: A clever man, untrustworthy. Suspected of pro-Nazi views, although he is too clever to show it in public. Would be capable of undercover or illegal activity.

Russell EVANS: One of Paul HAEGE's satellites, at HAEGE's beck and call. Director of Simpson Hain Pty Ltd. Most untrustworthy.

Margot ADAMS: Secretary to Simpson Hain Pty Ltd. Originally secretary to Paul HAEGE; one of HAEGE's most trusted persons. Originally thought HAEGE would marry her, but on finding out that it was not possible, moved her attractions to Dr. David MARTYN. Very loyal to Paul HAEGE and Alys MAIER. Could never be trusted as a contact.

Dr. David MARTYN: Dr. MARTYN holds a most vital position in the technical side of the war effort and his position is classified as most secret. His association with the people mentioned, whose views he must know, as his contact with them has been over a period of four years, is in itself to say the least, tactless.

The contact advises me that last Friday evening, in the present of Margot ADAMS, he discussed certain technicalities of Radar work, but only used technical terms. It is suggested that his association with these people be fully investigated as leakage of information concerning his duties and his knowledge could be most dangerous, and if anything was forthcoming that he was divulging any information, measures could be taken to point out to him the seriousness of his association with these people.

Alys Lee MAIER: German national of Chinese origin, married to Karl MAIER, internee. Described as the

> *cleverest of them all by HAEGE. Cunning type, who makes use of any men that are considered helpful to her. Could be classed as very immoral when it suits her.*
>
> *This woman has been the subject of many and varied investigations but to date has been able to keep her head above water. In this particular case, her close association with people such as Paul HAEGE, Russell EVANS, Margot ADAMS and Dr. David MARTYN, render her a security risk.*

Although Hargrave knew each of his protagonists' habits, their inner lives remained a mystery. There were several pertinent documents in the file; a statement from a plumber who found German photos and letters in the incinerator of a building the Maiers lived in, a note from the officer who had confiscated Christmas lights from the Balogh residence at Bellevue Hill, outlining how the lights might be used to send signals across the harbour—or worse, to enemy vessels. The most damning document in the file was a 1941 letter from a George Newton Kenworthy, an architect to whom Alys Maier had attempted to sell a magazine subscription.

> *Suppose Britain loses the war, what then do you think will happen to Australia?' Maier probed Kenworthy. 'In my position I come in contact with a number of prominent men and 95% of them are of the opinion that Australia would be better under German rule …*

Alys Maier was in an extraordinary position to circulate defeatist propaganda. Through the New York-based Union Circulation Company she had ample opportunity to syphon intelligence to contacts in the US and beyond, and as a distributor she had every excuse to travel throughout the city converting strangers. It was hard to imagine a woman better suited to being a spy. Her charm was notorious, her relationships varied and utilitarian—her ethics, quite possibly non-existent.

When Hargrave was assigned the case, he had been fresh faced and determined to put Maier behind bars. He and his team had taken every possible action, even going abroad for the latest in surveillance technologies. The investigation would go down in history as the very first telephone tapping and bugging operation in Australia and it was imperative their efforts yield results. The Security Service inserted informants among the Haege set, microphones were placed in Alys Maier's flat in the Danmark building, and agents were installed in the apartment directly above. But she and Balogh seemed to speak in code, their conversations were muffled and broken. Hargrave's early enthusiasm was fast dwindling.

He watched as Balogh emerged from the apartment block and walked to his waiting Pontiac. Tail-lights blazed and the car disappeared up Wolseley Road until the street was dark once more. Hargrave didn't bother to follow the suspect home to Bellevue Hill. Tomorrow morning he would hear from his agents stationed above Maier's apartment. Tonight was a wash, the same as all the others. There was no point lingering in Point Piper, it was time he got back to the office and began preparing his report for the Deputy Director.

Security Service, 117 Pitt Street, Sydney. 15th February, 1944.

Deputy Director of Security SYDNEY

SUBJECT: Union Circulation Coy and Victoria Trading Coy.

(Trading as General Merchants.)

On resuming the survey it was found that the association between Alys Maier of Union Circulation Coy and Andrew Balogh of Victoria Trading Coy was far more than a normal business association.

Firstly: Alys is living in a flat rented by Balogh in Wolseley Road, Point Piper, rental £6.6.0 per week. The flat shows Andrew Balogh as the tenant, but Alys Maier is living there and not Balogh, who resides at Drumalbyn Road, Bellevue Hill.

Alys Maier, at the moment, is on a bond of £30 for failing to notify change of address. Her present address is shown as Thompson St., Artarmon, but as already pointed out, she is living at Point Piper.

Socially, these two are closely connected with:–

1. Dr. David Martyn

2.Margot Adams. (see previous report—association with Paul Haege).

Andrew and Shan-Yi Balogh, photographed in Venice on their first world tour in 1954.

Andrew and Shan-Yi Balogh ride an elephant, 1954.

Shan-Yi Balogh, age thirty-seven, and Cora Lee, age thirty, reunite in New York, February 1954.

OSLO **Dagbladet** TIRSDAG 9. JULI 1957

14-meters flybillett for å reise rundt jorden

Australiere til Oslo med verdens lengste flybillett

Med en 14 meters flybillett i spesiallaget koffert, er det mulig å reise verden rundt. Turen tar 10 måneder og går innom 105 hovedsteder og 35 land, pluss at 28 flyselskaper kommer inn i bildet.

Australieren Mr. Andrew Balogh og hans kinesiskfødte kone Shanyi, har nå kommet til Oslo. De har vært på reisefot siden november, og har sett det meste av verden siden de forlot Sydney. Det er deres annen jordomseiling og den første i 1954 hadde gitt mersmak. Ekteparet rakk ikke oppom Skandinavia på sin første tur, men nå skal de ta igjen det forsømte med et tre ukers opphold i Norge. Mr. Balogh er tilknyttet importbusiness, og har ikke særlige problemer med finansene. Selv kunne han ikke i farten si hvor meget en tur verden rundt vil koste, det kommer jo an på hvilken måte man reiser. Torsdag kom han direkte fra Moskva, forbløffet over hvor rolig befolkningen tok den politiske omveltningen. Mest imponert var han over russernes gode service og menykart på 10 sider.

(Fortsatt side 8.)

Pengelotteriets trekningsliste

14 meter . . .

(Fortsatt fra side 1.)

Han kunne berette nytt fra alle verdens kanter, om et spillecasino i Argentina som var så stort at hele Monte Carlo kunne flyttes inn i et av rommene. Han for over verdenskartet i korte trekk, fortalte om herlige dager på Cuba, spennende opplevelser i Hong Kong, samt hvor hyggelig det var å se Kontikiflåten på Bygdøy.

Et norsk reisebyrå har lagt opp Norges-turen, med besøk på Vestlandet og hurtigrute opp til midnattsol og sommer. Mr. Balogh har selv lagt opp reiseruten, og alt i fjor kontaktet han det norske reisebyrået. I de store internasjonale flyrutebøkene er han kjent som i sin egen lomme, og sjekker avganger og ankomster uten hjelp i byråer. Han og hans frue gleder seg til å se de norske fjordene, som de bare hittil har sett på film. Han tviler nesten på at det kan være så vakkert. Etter Norges-visitten går turen via Danmark til Canada, for han rakk ikke oppom der tidligere på året.

Nå priser han seg lykkelig over å ha kommet helskinnet fra Russland, før han reiste spøkte vennene med at han kom til å havne i Sibir. Det er ingen Marco Polo reise ekteparet Balogh gjør, til gjengjeld har de strev med sin 14 meter lange billetter og reiseruter over alle hav og verdensdeler.

WORLD TOUR

MRS. ANDREW BALAGH, of Bellevue Hill, left Mascot today with her importer husband by Pan American Stratoclipper on a six months' world tour.

LONDON
Daily Telegraph and Morning Post.

33ft TRAVEL TICKET

Mr. Roland Hill, director of a travel bureau in Sydney, Australia, disputed yesterday a Tokyo travel agency report that it had issued the world's longest airline ticket. "We issued a 33ft long ticket for a Mr. and Mrs. Andrew Balogh, of Sydney, to travel by 28 airlines and visit 105 cities in 33 countries," he said. — B.U.P.

— A világ leghosszabb repülőgép-jegyét a sidneyi repülőgép-pénztárnál adták ki. A világkörüli útra szóló repülőjegy 9,9 méter hosszú. Tulajdonosa a magyar származású Balogh András és neje.

AZ EMBER

"GOING PLACES," Sydney Sun, 14/11/56, quotes:

"Mr. A. Balogh, a Sydney businessman, and his wife are going to visit 105 towns in 33 countries and are travelling by 28 airlines. Airline officials said it was the biggest airline booking ever arranged in Australia."

The entire arrangements regarding this exceptional travel

"SYDNEY MORNING HERALD" 15.11.1956

TICKETS FOR WORLD TRIP

Mr. and Mrs. Andrew Balogh, of Sydney, proudly hold up their 33ft tickets before boarding their plane at Mascot yesterday. They will travel on 28 airlines and visit 105 towns in 33 countries on what airline officials describe as the most extensive trip ever arranged in Australia.

Lima, Domingo 16 de Diciembre de 1956

Australiano llega a Lima con boletos aéreos que miden 11 metros de largo

Andrew Balough y señora... un largo viaje como el largo de sus boletos...

Los boletos con un largo de 11 metros que llevaba el señor Andrew G. Balogh, comerciante de Sydney, Australia llamaron la atención a los recepcionistas del mostrador, porque el viajero australiano en compañia de su esposa, está viajando con ellos desde que salió desde Australia.

A su llegada, declaró que está efectuando un viaje alrededor del mundo y ha venido a Lima, alentado por las perspectivas comerciales que ofrece en diversos aspectos. También que a la vez aprovechar la visita para cumplir un programa de turista, ya que escuchó mucho hablar de nuestro país, en su lejano continente. El señor Balogh, llegó en "El Inter—Americano" después de haber recorrido Africa, Europa, Medio Oriente y Asia y sus boletos que le permiten viajar a través de 105 ciudades de 33 diferentes países, se encuentran unidos para facilitar su desglosamiento.

Tickets—33 feet of them

Andrew Balogh waved his hands in despair at Mascot today when he got his tickets mixed up—all 33 feet of them.

But his pretty wife Shanyi quickly sorted things out, and explained the confusion to reporters.

Mr. Barogh, a Sydney importer, and his wife are going to visit 105 towns in 33 countries and are travelling by 28 airlines.

Airline officials said it was the biggest airline booking ever arranged for a passenger in Australia.

The Baroghs had to buy a special suitcase before they left on a Qantas Superconstellation for US.

There just wasn't room in the luggage for the tickets and paper.

"But by the time we've travelled for a little we won't have so many to worry about," Mr. Barogh said.

自本报编辑部6月14日发表"文

分子应当睁眼看看这些

JUST FANCY THAT...

CLAIM by a Tokyo travel agency that it had issued the world's longest airline ticket was disputed yesterday by Mr. Roland Hill, director of a Sydney travel bureau.

The Tokyo claim was that a 25ft.-long ticket was issued for a ... from Tokyo to the United States via 74 cities in Asia, Australia, South Africa, and Europe.

Said Mr. Hill: "Last November we issued a 33ft.-long ticket for Mr. and Mrs. Andrew Balogh, of Sydney. They travelled on 28 airlines and visited 105 cities in 33 countries."

AZ EMBER

...kezét, bravuros torontoi teljesítményükért . . . Ausztráliában most sokat beszélnek **Balogh Andrew**-ról, aki valamikor a pesti "8 Órai Ujság" utazási irodáját vezette, de aki 1939-ben kiment Sydneybe és ott egyik legnagyobb export-import vállalat tisztelt és mindenki által nagyrabecsült tulajdonosa lett. **Balogh** — nagyszerű tollú, kínai ujságírónő feleségével, — 1956 nov. 15-én repülő világkörüli utra indult, ahonnan 1957 aug. 20-án érkezett vissza. A Pan American repülőtársaságnál megnyerte a "világ leghosszabb repülőut-jegytulajdonosa"-nak címét, minthogy összeragasztott repülőjegy-sorozata 11 métert tett ki! A szerencsésen megérkezett Balogh-házaspárt most szeretettel ünneplik a Sydney-i magyarok és ausztrálok egyaránt.

Clippings from global newspapers published in 1956 and 1957, detailing Shan-Yi and Andrew Balogh's world tour and world record making 14-metre-long airline tickets.

Alys and Karl Maier enjoying the sailboat 'Volita' with friends on Sydney Harbour in 1939.

Alys Maier in Sydney working as a saleswoman for the Union Circulation Company.

Siblings Marie Lee Lew, Shan-Yi Balogh, Bob Lee and Cora Au stand behind their parents Poon Wong and Yee Lee to celebrate the couple's sixtieth wedding anniversary in Honolulu, 1968.

Shan-Yi Balogh alighting a plane during her travels with Andrew Balogh, 1960.

Shan-Yi Balogh with her mother, Poon Wong Lee, in Hong Kong, April 1962.

Sisters Shan-Yi Balogh, Marie Lee Lew and Cora Au celebrate Christmas in Honolulu, 1963.

Andrew and Shan-Yi Balogh holding newborn great-granddaughter Michelle Balogh, 1988.

Left to right: Albin, Diana, Michelle, Shan-Yi and Tristan Balogh, celebrating Tristan's ninth birthday in Summer Hill, 1999.

Shan-Yi Balogh, age seventy, in Chatswood, 1986.

Shan-Yi Balogh at Sydney International Airport, waiting in style to greet her sister Cora.

Shan-Yi, Michelle and Tristan Balogh celebrating Christmas in Summer Hill, 1994.

Shan-Yi Balogh, age ninety, and Michelle Balogh, eighteen, celebrating Shan-Yi's ninetieth birthday in Double Bay, 2006.

Martyn's association with them is hard to understand. He has been classed as 100% loyal, yet his knowledge of "Radar" locations, which is considered one of the most vital and secret in Navy and Air Force to-day, and also his known susceptibility to women, does not seem to blend. He has entertained both these people in his flat, and is not anxious for other friends of his to see them there. This was proved by a visit of a friend while they were at the flat. He contacts Alys at her office by 'phone and is apparently aware of any transactions these two are interested in, reference 'phone conversation 11.2.44, from Alys to David, when dummy names were used. If David Martyn did not know the meaning of this conversation why should Alys use them to him?

Balogh's associates are many and varied and general opinion of him by people associated with him in Hungary is that he is an unscrupulous type who would stoop to anything to further his own ends. So the combination of the two is rather ideal in their own set-up.

The general method of conducting his business needs mention as night time seems to be the main time for any transactions and arrangements he wants to make.

Firstly, (although not a security matter) his allowance is 4 gallons per month. Yet in five days he covered 138 miles, mostly at night time.

He is supposed to be dealing in semi-precious stones imported from India under licence. Surely this would not entail night travelling and from what I am told stones are hard to distinguish at night time.

It is quite possible that Balogh is setting up a "refugee" trade for post war in the jewellery business and is adopting rather unusual methods to say the least to further his interests. Alys Maier may also be interested from that angle.

It has not been possible to date to glean a great deal from 'phone conversations, and most of the conversations that matter appear to be in riddle form or in a special wording of their own.

His movements by car at night have been followed and his unusual method of leap-frogging backwards and forwards between two or three places at night lead one to suspect something, but what it is hard to determine.

Balogh's general 'phone conversations are not by any means of a normal type.

It has to be definitely decided before it can be classed as completed:–

1. What is the reason of the association of Dr. David Martyn?

2. Is Paul Haege in some way connected with Balogh?

3. Is Balogh outside Security in that he is "Black Marketing"?

As will be realised puzzling features run through this case and a further report will be submitted when something more definite is reached.

New York

When Tom was ignoring me and I most needed a friend, Natalia returned to Sydney. I'd known her since high school but we were never especially close back then—just casual friends, running in the same circles. But she returned from two years of study in Italy right when I was itching for company—right at the time when I realised what a miracle it is to make a new friend. She needed to start over her life in Sydney, so we decided to start over our friendship.

It was easy to talk to Natalia, especially since she'd been gone so long. There was no expectation that we would know anything about one another's lives—no guilt surrounding the fact that it had been so long since we'd last caught up. Over time the small talk morphed into big talk, and soon we were spending long nights together, gossiping over two-for-one cocktails. Out of all of our friends, we were the two who were single—the two who hadn't quite figured out where our lives were headed. We both loved getting dressed up and going new places, we liked yoga and music festivals and costume parties. Together we wove our lives around one another. And so, I was gifted with the one thing I needed most in the world—an unconditional girlfriend.

It was springtime in New York City but it felt like winter. In Central Park, mounds of ploughed snow had yet to melt, the sky was clear, but the air bit at my cheeks. Walking down Fifth Avenue, Natalia and I got caught in the Easter Parade—fancy dress and bonnets shaped like bunnies. We'd decided to explore New York and Los Angeles, to spend a year's savings on swaying to music under the palm trees of Coachella, before I headed up to Yale to see Tom for the first time in months.

After a week of eating, drinking and sightseeing, Natalia and I parted at Grand Central Station and I boarded the train up to New Haven. As the train wound from New York to Connecticut, the scenery was a blur of winter greys. I was nervous, imagining the reunion with Tom in a million different incarnations. I caught a cab from Union Station to his flat at Wooster Square. Waiting at the doorstep, I looked up and down the street. Despite our months of video chat, it was jarring to see his home in person. He'd made a new life in this subdivided weatherboard house. I shifted on the spot and fiddled with my hair, and then he was standing before me, flesh and blood.

Inside, we made awkward circles around one another

as he prepared tea. He ushered me into his bedroom to put down my things. Looking around the space that I had seen in so many photos, I wondered how well I would fit into it. I wanted to stay, to be part of the stark white room. The bed stood between us, speaking without words.

For three days everything was simple. The town softened as we ate pizza and drank wine, as we wandered around the frosty campus after dark. The days were ice cold. I was bundled up in a scarf and gloves when he showed me his desk in the classics library, leading me in weaving lines between the rows of shelves. When he introduced me to his peers he placed his hand on my lower back. He smiled as he played the tour guide, whispered commentary into my ear when no-one was watching.

At night we spooned in bed and barely slept. I fell asleep in a library while I waited for him to finish class. I tried to explore the art gallery while my eyes fluttered open and closed. He said we were living in a 'heterocosm'—a temporary world of our own, far from the consequences that surrounded us in Sydney. I called him a wanker, but he was right—New Haven was a bubble. For three days, nobody else existed.

I brought Tom back to New York with me to meet up with Natalia but as soon as we arrived, everything was different. We went out for drinks that first night, flitting between *Lonely Planet*'s favourite bars, but when I put my arm around

Tom, he brushed it away. When I stood too close he grumbled and frowned. He refused to be mistaken for a couple and begrudged my acting intimate around Natalia.

She brought Sydney to New York with her, and his every action changed.

The two people I loved most niggled and butted heads, disagreed about where to go and what to do. He was controlling and bossy, taking ownership of the city—always wanting to lead the way. Her hackles were raised by his intellectual demeanour, his haughty lectures and use of fancy words. She argued and nit-picked, but I could see that her grievances ran deeper. She didn't trust him, didn't like the way that he treated me. I tried to stretch my friendship to encircle all three of us, but still we bickered. When we returned to the hotel, I was glad to be back in a room with just Natalia but a deep ache filled my chest. Something special was slipping away.

The following day we went out for breakfast and walked along the High Line. It was sunny and bright, the cold was melting away, but the city wasn't the same as it had been the week before. The infinite possibilities of a Manhattan street were reduced to the space between Tom and me, and the possibilities between us were numbered.

We rode to the top of the Empire State Building and while Tom and Natalia took pictures, positioning their iPhones against gaps in the safety cage, I walked around the top of the tower unable to see the city. I was exhausted by travel, exhausted by my feelings—I was crumbling in slow motion. I may have been up in the clouds but my heart was buried deep below the subway. Riding back down in the dim elevator, I kept my sunglasses on. No one would see my tears.

When I followed Tom back to his hotel room that night, my heart was in my throat. Lying on the single bed together, I wanted to reach into him and *make* him want me. But when I leant towards him, he lurched from my embrace.

'You're here because you're in love with me,' he said. 'But I'm only here because I want to have sex.'

Albin

Shan-Yi and Albin, Andrew's ten-year-old son, were both testing the water. They extended kindnesses to one another and then shrunk backwards, each waiting to see if the gesture was returned. She was reminded of dogs meeting in the street, sniffing and encircling one another, protective of their territory. Steadily growing closer.

In September of 1944, the two of them holidayed in the little beachside town of Jervis Bay, south of Sydney. Andrew was busy with business and suggested that Shan-Yi and Albin go together—the school holidays were a good opportunity for her to get to know his son. Despite her caution, Shan-Yi wanted the boy to like her. Albin still spent time with his mother, Boëske, who lived just across the harbour in Sydney—but it was with his father that he lived full-time, just up the road from Scots College, where he went to school. If Shan-Yi were to have a future with Andrew, they needed to become family.

She wore her broadest smile and listened with interest to the stories that Albin had to tell. During their first few days she often talked about Andrew, wanting Albin to see how much she loved his father. But after a while she noticed the hurt in the boy's tightened lips whenever she talked about 'Daddy'—the hurt she caused by implying she might prefer the father to the son. She read *The Troublesome Boy* and, as far as studies in child psychology went, found it fairly interesting—but none of it seemed to apply to Albin. He was the least troublesome boy she had ever met.

The pair went for walks along the white sands of Hyams Beach and explored the neighbouring bushland. They collected shells and wildflowers, pointed out crabs and blue bottles. When Shan-Yi found a tiny orchid, perfect in its detail and no more than an inch wide, she brought it back to the hotel room and placed it in a glass. She was surprised by how well they got along. At twenty-eight years old she didn't know much about little boys, but most of the time Albin didn't act like one. She couldn't decide whether his pleasures were abnormally grown up, or if hers were childish. Either way, he seemed to like her, although she could see that he had his frustrations. One day he wanted to visit the nearby Royal Australian Naval College, HMAS Creswell, but Shan-Yi refused. When a gentleman at the College House Hotel sent a bottle of champagne to their table at dinner one night, Albin was appalled when Shan-Yi sent it right back.

Andrew wrote to them every day. They slept in late and waited for the mail to arrive at ten o'clock, delaying their walk until his letter arrived. The letters were always addressed to Albin and written in Hungarian. As they walked along the beach, Albin would carefully translate his father's words, but Shan-Yi wished that Andrew would write to her directly. It hurt to see him favour his son, although she knew that it was the right thing to do. Every day she wrote a letter back and asked Andrew to reply in English, even though she knew he was embarrassed by his clumsiness with the language. When Albin went to sleep she read his father's letters again, puzzling over the words.

She was determined to learn the language and sat with Albin on the rocks with her copy of *Berlitz Hungarian*. The waves lapped at their feet while they recited verb conjugations. The boy was a good teacher and his unselfconscious methods yielded surprising results. He made her repeat words over and over again and his insistence that she get them right made for quicker progress than Andrew's patient flattery. She looked forward to showing off her new vocabulary when she got home.

Two days before they were due to leave, they received one final letter.

> *Forgive me this short, stupid and primitiv letter and I am ashame my self, because I whant to write you quite different thing, but I must write what I think I can spellit.*

It was the most beautiful thing Shan-Yi had ever seen.

Mrs Balogh

Shan-Yi helped plan her friends Margot and David Forbes Martyn's wedding, all the while wishing that it was her own. It was 1944 and she couldn't stay married to Karl, not for the duration of a war that seemed interminable. It was time she became Mrs Andrew Balogh. It was time she got a divorce.

Their letters crossed paths, somewhere in the vast countryside of New South Wales or Victoria. Karl wrote to Shan-Yi, congratulating Margot and David and reminding her of the summer morning long ago in Bombay when they wed. She sent him a letter at precisely the same time, reminding him of something else entirely.

> *I have heard a story shocking beyond words, and yet explaining clearly so much of the unhappiness in our life together. I see at last, that the basis of all our quarrels*

> *and difficulties did not lie—as you so consistently and unscrupulously argued—in my suspiciousness or petty-mindedness, but in your years' long string of infidelities, and your need (as it seemed to you) to deceive me about them.*

The war of letters raged on for weeks. They each anticipated the other's words—fighting a second set of arguments, limited to the imagination. Shan-Yi detailed Karl's infidelities as though they had only just been uncovered. Concealing her own relationship with Andrew, she insisted that her husband provide a full account of his actions. But he shirked the blame, painting the women with whom he was intimate as 'foolish' and 'cruel'. She was discouraged by his spite-filled explanations, unappeased by the way he sneered at his mistresses. Yes, these women were supposed to have been her 'best friends', but she could not forget that he was her *husband*. When he begged her not to call the women and press them for their own accounts, her mind was filled with even more suspicion.

All the while, Karl continued to fume about Shan-Yi's dalliance with Charlie Jones. For all the time she had thought Karl magnanimous, it appeared that he had only forgiven her transgression under the belief that it was an act of retaliation. Now that he knew she had been ignorant of his own adultery, he was filled with new-found rage over hers.

> *That I forgave you instantly and I blamed only myself, although you had committed adultery, shows clearly that*

I considered your action a sequel to your knowledge of my infidelity. That is why I will not accept now to be branded as the sole culprit.

Understand that if you ever wish a divorce, it must be by mutual consent. You will not get one step further the way you are now going about it. Unless it is by mutual consent I shall fight tooth and nail not to lose you, because I love you. I want to know who has come into your life.

Karl's letters alternated between anger and professions of love. Reminding her of their most precious memories, he wove a perfect story of the years they spent together. In florid prose he insisted that she was the only woman he had ever truly loved.

Shan-Yi wept over the letters, but she never wavered in her decision. She had fought for so long to win love and sincerity from Karl, and perhaps she finally had them. But even in the rare moments when his words clutched at her heart, the pleasure was spoiled by distrust. Perhaps she could forgive his infidelity, but she could never forgive his dishonesty. The thought that he was able to lie to her—time and time again, without scruple—filled her with horror.

The misery of fighting Karl fuelled her love for Andrew. She was reminded what she was fighting for and gained a greater appreciation for what she now had. As for Andrew, he was anxious she might have a change of heart. He was a worry wart, but she loved him for it. She engulfed his nervousness in her tiny arms, held him close and kissed his cheeks. It would all be over soon.

You accused me of looking too avidly for the bad to see the good. Don't think that. I have not forgotten the love we've had all these years, even if most of it lay only in my own romanticism. After all, so much of life is no more than that.

There is just one thing … as a young girl, I conceived an ideal of love which even this hasn't killed. If you cannot fulfil it—and you have given me no reason to think that you will—I prefer going on alone, even if I am to find it in no one else. Whatever happens, my dear, I wish you happiness with all my heart.

Karl was released from internment in Tatura and placed into the Civil Alien Corps starting work in late 1944. He was a labourer under the Property and Survey Branch of the Department of the Interior, working in forestry around Cotter Damn near Canberra. When he finally could return to Sydney, he tried to salvage his marriage once more.

One evening, Andrew drove Shan-Yi to Karl's flat and remained in the car, watching through the window as Karl fell to his knees, desperate in his pleas to reconcile. When the couple moved away from the window and out of sight, Andrew's imagination worked through every possible worst-case scenario. By the time Shan-Yi returned to the car, he was almost faint with fear that she might leave him. She had no intention of this, but her husband was not going to make it easy. In June 1945, their domestic battle made the pages of the *Mirror* newspaper.

Chinese Wife Ordered Back

A German who was interned in Australia for three and a

half years is working for the Department of the Interior at Canberra, according to evidence in the Divorce Court today.

He is Karl August Maier (37) King's Cross, who obtained a court order directing his Chinese wife Alys Virginia Maier (28) Wolseley Rd, Point Piper, to return to him within 21 days.

Maier said he was an agent for English book publishing firms before his internment in 1941, and that his wife worked for him in his business.

After his release some months ago, said Maier, his wife refused to live with him, although she agreed to continue working for him.

Maier said he now had a job with the Department of the Interior at Canberra.

The legal process dragged on, but ultimately Shan-Yi was granted a divorce. It was a different article that she clipped from the newspaper and secured carefully into a white satin album, surrounded by photographs. One that came a year later, in *The Sunday Sun*, 17 November 1946.

Bless You

Friends of Andrew Balogh and lovely Shan-Yi (pronounced Shaan-Yee) Lee, who dropped by for a cocktail at Andrew's home realised they were really bidden to the wedding reception of this charming pair.

Shan-Yi looked a dream in a French clocque semi-formal, and prompted linguist Theodore Barry to tell her in Chinese, 'God bless you, darling.' To Andrew he said, in Hungarian, 'It delights my heart.'

Physicist from Canberra, Dr. David Martyn, whose main charm is his polished simplicity, voiced our general joy in one of the most sincere speeches I've yet heard.

Blame

Shan-Yi had been gone for two and a half years.

I watched water run from the kitchen tap, splattering against the metal sink, oppressive thoughts rooting me to the spot. I fought against the feelings of worthlessness, but they followed me through my days. I drove to the library to work on my writing, to try to take a fresh step towards my goals. But as I pulled into the carpark, I was too tired to go inside, too tired to do anything. When I woke two hours later, still sitting in the car, my mouth was dry, my skin slicked with sweat. I turned around and drove back home again.

The more weeks passed, the harder it became to function. My body was leaden, my mind rerunning the same old thoughts about Tom, Flair and the grim financial consequences of an American holiday paid for on credit card. I felt defeated by my efforts. All I wanted was to do something with my time that was rewarding, that made me happy and contributed something to the world. But my short-lived career at Flair was over, and the last two and a half years of perceived progress seemed to have come to nothing. But it wasn't about a list of grievances—I could feel my sadness slipping away from the experiences that first set it in motion.

Sometimes sadness gave way to anger, to a fury that served as fuel in itself. I could derive energy from anger. I was heartbroken, but I was angrier at Tom as a friend than I ever could be as a lover. I couldn't help but fixate on all of the times I had asked him for space—the times I said I was falling for him and he treated my words like white noise. Back then, I explained away his actions. I chose to believe he had feelings for me because it was easier than believing that my best friend didn't care much what I needed.

Couldn't he have turned to someone less broken? Wasn't there someone to fool around with who wasn't in love with him? In my darkest hours I thought about our first physical encounters and I wondered if I could ever truly forgive him. I filled sleepless nights with rage, with thoughts of all the things he had done. As painful as it was—as much as I tossed and turned—it was easier than falling apart over the things that *I* had done.

I thought about Shan-Yi chasing Karl around the globe, then settling down with Andrew. The course of her life was determined by marriage. She was a globetrotting, freewheeling adventuress, but every major turn she took could be plotted out by her relationships with men. Then again, she was building a life in the 1930s and 40s on the opposite side of the globe to her family. She had every reason to prioritise relationships—she needed safety and security and someone to depend on. What excuse did I have?

With the blinding clarity of hindsight, I could see how I contorted my mind to let Tom in. I allowed myself to fall in love. When I looked back, I couldn't decide if he had broken my heart or if I had done it for him. I settled for a relationship without the commitment I needed, prioritising the pursuit of being loved over finding strength in myself—willing to do anything in exchange for the feeling that somebody cared. For a single moment of that feeling, I made terrible decisions, selfish decisions. I collected memories to justify my actions, rearranged my thoughts to accommodate how I felt—the flutter in my chest whenever he was near. I focused on the times that his mother told me she wished we were together, all of the times new acquaintances asked if we were more than just friends. I focused on the cracks in Tom and Jessica's relationship and told myself all sorts of lies. I fooled around with a friend's boyfriend when I was smart enough to know that it was unforgiveable.

The story of how Shan-Yi uncovered Karl's string of infidelities was something I was never told but always just *knew*—such was its infamy among our family and friends. He was interned and she was given the key to the mailbox—that was how all of his affairs came to light. I had always felt sorry for Shan-Yi, fooled by a philandering husband. I wondered what type of blinkers it would take to shutter out that kind of infidelity. What lies would you have to tell yourself to be played like that—and by a Nazi, no less. But was I any better? Sure, I could draw a fierce line against anti-Semitism and white supremacy—my political views didn't hinge on a man and I knew not to simply adopt my partner's perspective. I might never be pressured in or out of an abortion in the way that Shan-Yi was, but I let Tom treat my body like a commodity in his own quiet way.

I always thought I should look up to Shan-Yi because she was fierce and sassy. Because she was a ball-buster who was glamorous and beautiful and wild. She lived her life with tenacity—but that didn't mean she always made the right choices. And it didn't mean that I should live a life like hers. Shan-Yi grew into womanhood at a time when her body wasn't her own, when opportunity was scarce, and when her next choice was one of survival. I had opportunity, privilege, and independence—but what did I have to show for it?

Mother

During the months and years of waiting to be married, Shan-Yi and Andrew spoke often of the children they would have together, but now that the time had finally come, they had little to show for their efforts. Shan-Yi's body was failing her—her pregnancies were short-lived. She went to the doctor and could feel the tears welling in her eyes before she even made it into the office. But there was no point surrendering, she wasn't one to cry and fret. She was determined to get what she came for.

The doctor pursed his lips as she outlined her medical history—the times she had fallen pregnant to Karl; the times he had asked her to end it. She could see the disapproval etched across his face, but still she continued. She had come for answers. The doctor put her through a battery of tests, but the verdict was stark.

'You won't have children. You won't be able to carry a child.'

Andrew cried with her when they received the prognosis, but it was easier for him—he already had a son. His mind didn't race; he didn't feel the frustration coursing through his veins. Shan-Yi raged against Karl, raged against her own body. She stood in the dressing room that Andrew had built for her, bathed in the golden light that once made her feel a queen, and stared at her figure—the tiny frame had always served her well. Her body had seen her through thirty-one years, traversing land and sea. It was the face that was photographed a thousand times, the figure that men complimented. But now it was a leaden weight.

As the years slid out from under Shan-Yi, Albin became her son. She walked the boy to school in the mornings, fed him his dinner at night. She challenged him and encouraged him, expressed her love through scolding and teasing and poetry. They were a family, building a life together on Drumalbyn Road, Bellevue Hill. Shan-Yi's husband and son were happy and healthy—they didn't see her at three in the morning, when she woke in a sweat. She moved between Andrew and Albin with ease, but her dreams were still full of children—the children she would never have.

The Guinness Book

Shan-Yi's second marriage was as much defined by distance as her first. Andrew was often away as he travelled the world, visiting trade fairs from Tokyo to Hamburg, selecting goods to import to Sydney. But waiting at home for him didn't feel the same as waiting for Karl. Shan-Yi missed her husband, but she didn't worry. She ached for him to return, but she never questioned that he would.

When she divorced Karl, she began working for Andrew at the Victoria Trading Company, helping with the administrative work alongside a team of three or four others in the city. Over time, Andrew granted her more responsibility and while she wasn't the office manager, she might as well have been.

Whenever Andrew was overseas she wrote to him daily, some days more than once. Bent over her typewriter at the dining table, the teenaged Albin sitting opposite her, working through his maths equations and Latin conjugations. After his homework was done, he would make models—electrical trains that travelled along fine tracks and every kind of aeroplane. He painted each of the pieces himself, dozens of tiny plastic people, railway stations, and all different kinds of trees. The miniature world could keep him occupied for hours, but whatever time he went to bed, Shan-Yi would still be typing.

Andrew couldn't match her non-stop correspondence, but he wrote home whenever he could. Shan-Yi waited back in the city after work, visiting the post office before and after dinner in hope of finding a letter in the box. Andrew wrote to her in Hungarian and his adult nephew, Lorand, translated the letters. He wrote of coming face to face with temptation in Japan, of trying to conceal the bulge in his pants while receiving a massage at an exclusive club for businessmen. Lorand was mortified and appalled, gushing apologies on behalf of his uncle, but Shan-Yi laughed and wrote back asking what he'd done to ease the tension. Her husband was honest and open, there was a trust that came with sharing all. When Andrew grew tired of having their communications witnessed, he began to send her cassette tapes in his broken English, recording his thoughts from the privacy of hotel beds—blankets draped over his head, nervous of being heard.

Sometimes Shan-Yi felt lonely, but she wasn't alone—apart from Albin, she had a large extended family and often spent weekends with Lorand and his wife in Campsie among a tight-knit community of Hungarian friends and relatives. They would all go together to the airport when Andrew left on his travels, waving up at the aeroplane as it made its roaring ascent. She wore her brightest red dress and stood on the observation platform until the plane was all the way out of sight, hoping he could see her from the sky.

Andrew and Shan-Yi were married for almost a decade before they made their first international trip together. A decade of planning and dreaming, of saving and imagining all of the places they would go. When the time came, in 1954, Albin was twenty and studying at the University of Sydney, making it an ideal time for them to travel as a couple. Andrew called himself meticulous, Shan-Yi called him neurotic—either way, their itinerary was designed with extreme care.

Two years later in 1956, a second world trip would put the first to shame. It was a behemoth, a feat of the modern era, a journey that spanned the globe. For Shan-Yi, the thought of reuniting with so many of their family and friends, of showing Andrew many of the places that sculpted her into the woman that she was made her giddy. In the weeks leading up to their departure she barely slept. She was itching to visit new places, to explore North and South America, to travel through Africa and Asia, through every city in Europe that she had ever wished to see.

The press came to the airport at Mascot to see them off. A photographer snapped pictures as they grappled with their fourteen-metre-long airline tickets, a length of paper issued for each leg of the journey. The pictures were published in the *Sydney Morning Herald*, and then travelled further, circulating around the world. In newspapers from Russia to China their name was spelled every which way—Balough, Barogh, Balagh. The misspellings were varied but the story was always the same—the couple officially had the longest airline tickets in the world. When their names were published in *The Guinness Book of Records* the following year, Andrew bought copies for everyone they knew.

Shan-Yi documented the trip for Albin, keeping her son well versed in all the adventures she embarked on with 'Dad'.

> *We had a marvellous trip across the Atlantic but were unable to enjoy it, having been practically unconscious after two weeks of New York. The "President Special" is, I understand, the most luxurious of flights, and we were offered not only a wonderful dinner, but everything else free—cigarettes, champagne, liqueurs, and liquors of every kind right until dinner; Dad woke me for that, but I fell asleep again right after soup… They played soft music all evening and the stewards wore white dinner jackets and black tie and looked fearfully elegant—but the condition I was in I wouldn't have batted an eyelid had they been in sackcloth and ashes. However, I did get my share of the orchid and bottle of French perfume with which every female passenger was presented upon arrival in London. N.B.—when you board a flight you walk on blue carpet between gleaming chromium hand-railings!!! Made me feel awfully silly when after all a plane is only a plane is only a plane is only a plane is only a plane a la Gertrude Stein—and all*

that's important is that the dratted thing stays up when it's supposed to.'

Andrew lugged his recording equipment everywhere they went, filming the lives and landscapes they encountered. Shan-Yi sometimes grew impatient with him, struggling through the airports with his camera, film reels, typewriter, documents, books and Shavemaster, but she was proud of his ingenuity. When they got home, they spent hours sitting side by side carefully recording commentary and applying sound effects before renting the local cinema to share their travels with family and friends.

Shan-Yi fell in love with Peru, with exploring Incan ruins and the rainforests that stretched on forever. Perhaps even more so trying her first tequila, lemon, and salt. She loved Mexico where they visited casinos along the coast, and was enthralled by the spectacle of bullfighting. She slept in over ninety different beds on that world tour but never grew weary, never wished to be home.

Darkness

Darlinghurst was a maze of winding alleys. Drinkers and smokers and pill-poppers stumbled through the night. Bright lights blotted out the stars, but that didn't matter when the locals' cheeks were covered in glitter. I liked the dreary grey streets lit up by neon signs, the rows of restaurants and bars, the gritty feel of neighbouring Kings Cross—the strip joints, kebab shops, and clubs with sticky floors. Sydney's lock-out laws might have worked to dim some of the area's colour, but there remained a vitality to my neighbourhood that would not be suppressed.

At night, when I couldn't sleep, I walked down to the harbour at Rushcutters Bay. The water was rippling ink, cut only by the lines of gold that dripped from lamps along the park. I sat on the sandstone wall, my feet hanging over the water, and waited for a voice to call out my name. Other times, I wove through the streets of Potts Point and

Elizabeth Bay, obsessed with the art-deco buildings, the European feel of the overgrown avenues. As I walked the streets I imagined Shan-Yi up there in one of the windows, typing into the night.

I liked living in Darlinghurst, but that was when I was out among it. Now I was confined to my basement flat, only leaving when the chime of the phone summoned me to another temp reception job. The rest of the time, I hid under my blankets. Not even the sun could creep inside, bend its way through to my underground bedroom.

I was seventeen when anxiety first gave way to depression. Having navigated through a childhood of fear and phobia, I was already an expert at putting on a good front—at living a dual life of mental illness and social normality. But depression was something new—I didn't recognise the disease for what it was when it came for me.

I recognised the symptoms now and had been taking medication for years and was glad for my anti-depressants, grateful for the help they provided in getting me through the day. I was grateful for my psychologist; with whom I'd booked a new batch of appointments. My parents were supportive as always, I had a childhood home to escape to. But counselling and medication and family weren't enough—even combined—they couldn't carry me on their own.

It's easier to climb out of depression when you're handed a glamorous apartment, when you're given the opportunity to disappear into another life. Picking myself up for the second time felt impossible—I felt as if there was no hope, that life was a series of hurdles that were way too high to leap across. Then I remembered the story of when my mum ran for her high school at the regional carnival in Gunnedah; she picked the hurdles up and threw them out of her way.

I started running again. I ran away from my worries like they were chasing me down the street. I remembered all the nights that I came home to Shan-Yi's apartment and lay sprawled out on her Persian rug in happy exhaustion. If it worked before, it could work again. A jog around the block wouldn't cure me, but it seemed like a decent place to start.

When I looked back on the distance I'd already come, I found other clues I could follow along the path to feeling better. I was happier as a temp receptionist than I ever had been working at Flair. All the champagne and finger food in the world couldn't make me love writing about makeup. So why was I always trying so hard *not* to be a receptionist? Why did I think I was too good for a job that made me happy?

I always thought that I was confident and bold, forging my own path. But so many of my thoughts were influenced by the opinions of others. I took the job in online publishing because it seemed glamorous, because it fed into the ideas I had of what my life *should* look like. When I told old friends that I was working as a receptionist, they peered at me in surprise. They asked if I was looking for better work—had I ever considered teaching? What about studying law? Everyone had an opinion.

It took me a long time to realise that mine was the only opinion that mattered. I had all the information I needed to know what was right for me. I needed to be around others and I couldn't work alone from home. I needed to be creative, but I wanted to pursue my own work telling stories that I was passionate about and felt were of value. I needed a steady income, I needed to feel secure and unafraid of falling into debt. If I added those pieces of information together, I could figure out what to do.

I applied for a permanent part-time reception role—a job-share at a large private healthcare company. I'd learnt that the companies I enjoyed working at most were the ones with a lot of people—it was hard enough to make friends as an adult, I needed to take every opportunity to be around potential friends. It was a well-paid position: I could cover my bills in five hours a day and the rest of the day was my own to pursue the work that was less financially rewarding, but gave me a sense of creative purpose. The balance would require a tight budget, but I could make it work.

I tried to be open with my friends, more explicit about my depression. If they knew what was going on, perhaps this time I could limit the fallout. When Tom returned to Sydney for the American summer, we tried to mend our friendship though we soon fell into old patterns, the lines between us were still blurred. I was always the one he turned to—he placed his worries into my hands, but I didn't have the strength left to support them. When he left for Yale again I was relieved. I asked that this time we ditch the texting and skyping and snapchat. But as soon as he landed he was at it again, sending me every homesick thought. I finally made a decision and told him the truth.

We couldn't be friends anymore. And as easy as that, I could breathe. I didn't miss him, didn't doubt my choice. I had put so much into our relationship over the last couple of years—my mind, my heart, my body—and now all those things were mine once more. I was happy to have them.

Less than six months later, when he announced his engagement to someone else, he didn't get in touch to tell me the news.

Years

It was New Year's Eve, the dawn of 1962, some forty-two years since Shan-Yi spent her first western new year quarantined at Seattle. Albin was twenty-eight and married to Margot Noseda, a fellow member of the theatre society at the University of Sydney. On the second day of the year, their first son Matthew Peter Balogh was born. Shan-Yi's grandson wasn't a cute baby, but she loved his expressions, was fascinated by the curious way he gazed around the room. She was certain he was intelligent. Shan-Yi and Andrew bought him presents and set up child-proof spaces in the Bellevue Hill apartment to make him feel at home. But they only played doting grandparents for two short years. Albin and Margot were too bohemian for clean-cut Sydney and in 1964 took Matt to Italy where they'd secured jobs as English teachers in Rome. They planned on staying a year.

Hiring a young English au pair, Sheila, to look after their son, they lived a laidback life in the centre of the city, rising whenever they woke, relaxing on the weekend over cigarettes and wine and pasta. But when the twelve months were up, the young family didn't return to Sydney. Having adjusted to life as Italians, they told Shan-Yi and Andrew they were staying put. As more years passed and Matt grew into a boy, they rarely visited; though they wrote often, sending news and photos, it wasn't the same. Shan-Yi was hurt that their son didn't want to be near them. Then again, she thought, he was the child they'd raised. If he was selfish, they only had themselves to blame.

She thought back on the day she had left Ellensburg as a teenager. She couldn't believe she had ever been so crazy, running away without any money, living in a strange city where anything could have happened. She had been so naive—stupid, really—and lucky that she hadn't been hurt or killed.

Rome was all blue skies and burnt gold stone, *suppli* for lunch and Campari in the late afternoon. But European pleasures weren't enough to save Albin and Margot's marriage. The couple divorced in 1971 and four years later Albin married a British girl from Ealing called Diana James. Albin and Diana met through the British Institute of Rome, where he taught English and she worked as an examiner. Their wedding was held at the Piazza del Campidoglio, a model train drove in circles on top of the chocolate wedding cake.

Albin's second marriage was followed by a second son,

Charles, who was born in December 1977. Charles' big brother Matt was fifteen by now and lived with his mother Margot in Geneva, Switzerland, where he attended the international high school. The Balogh clan was growing and Shan-Yi and Andrew were delighted by the birth of a second grandson even if they were all so far away.

Shan-Yi sent dozens of letters to Albin and Diana, encouraging them to move back to Sydney. She even sent letters to her son's ex-wife, pleading with her to come back with Matt. But while she received letters in return from them all, none made any promises.

For her parents' sixtieth wedding anniversary, Shan-Yi travelled to Honolulu with Andrew by her side. After the war, it took decades to secure Yee and Poon Wong's re-entry to the United States and all four Lee siblings had to work hard to extract their parents from China. But by the early 1960s they were together once more—Bob, Cora, Shan-Yi and Marie, Yee and Poon Wong. Seeing her parents was like being transported back to another life—she was forty-six, but she was just a child, desperate to fall into their arms.

Bob served as a second lieutenant in the United States Air Force, then opened his own pharmacy in Albuquerque, where he settled with his wife and children. Cora, a mother of four, raised her family in Honolulu where she was one of the state's first Chinese obstetrics gynaecologists. Mi and Marie had remained in Moscow, Idaho, running The Grill and becoming part of the fabric of the community. They hired students from the university to work as waitresses then watched them go off and marry, stopping by the café to visit as mothers and grandmothers. When Bob and Cora had returned to Moscow alone in 1937, the couple treated the children as their own, having never been able to conceive. Marie was married over a decade before a routine visit to the doctor resulted in the news that she was seven months pregnant. After her first baby Claire was born, four more children followed.

In many ways, Shan-Yi's immediate family were strangers, people who knew her better than anyone but didn't know her at all. Four siblings, separated by land and sea. She cuddled their babies and posed for photos, taking home dozens of images to treasure until the next reunion.

Back in Australia, Shan-Yi often stayed with Margot and David Martyn, who had moved down to the observatory at Stromlo in the ACT where David continued his research. Shan-Yi liked the bush around Canberra, the dry landscape and sweeping fields. She liked going down to their chicken coop with Margot to collect eggs in the morning and staying up late at night drinking wine by the fire with her old friends. But after a week, she was always ready to return to Sydney—to come home to Andrew, and her life. She no longer yearnt to travel, to see new places and write about her adventures.

David and Margot were family, she was familiar with all of their quarrels and their moments of joy. She loved them both more than almost anyone in the world. In March 1970, when the news came of David's suicide, she felt as though the stars had been stripped from the sky. Memories of nights spent together at the Stromlo observatory turned from glittered navy to pitch black. She stumbled about for days, a gaping hole reaching right through her.

Shan-Yi welcomed Margot into her home and they became roommates for months following David's death. The two women kept busy, scheduling activities every day, trying to behave like there wasn't something missing—like there wasn't a black cloud that followed them wherever they went. They spoke about David with reverence, discussing the awards he had won and recounting his contributions to the scientific community. But they avoided the minutiae of life in Stromlo and Camden, of his pointing out planets and constellations, of feeding native birds.

Decades later, a biographer chronicling the life and career of David Martyn visited the Balogh home and dumped a great pile of paper down on the coffee table before Shan-Yi. It was her file from the Australian Security Intelligence Organisation. Here was her life, narrated on page after page of surveillance reports. There were transcripts of conversations with Andrew, of words that passed between them while in bed. Agents wondered whether 'I'm going down to the wine shop, should I get one or two bottles of red?' was a reference to communism. There were countless times that she and Andrew worried they were being watched. They worried about the immigration department, particularly after she was reprimanded for failing to disclose a change of address. But not once had it crossed her mind that she might be considered a legitimate security threat.

For a moment she felt violated, disgusted by the thought of strangers listening in to the most intimate moments of her marriage; those early days of thrilling love, of long conversations over wine on the sofa, all the passionate words whispered by Andrew in broken English. But when that moment passed, she laughed. What an extraordinary waste of time. What a ridiculous waste of resources.

Sentiment

Without Flair or Tom to distract me, I finally sat and read through all Shan-Yi's letters—every single one. It took me weeks just to sort through them. I lay them out in chronological order, burying my flat under a blanket of paper. A snowfall of decades-old stories. The quantity of letters was startling, but it was the content that shocked me most. I found myself growing more and more bewildered the further I moved through her words.

The woman I watched in Dad's video was the Shan-Yi I always knew. Speaking without embellishment, ending each anecdote with 'and that was that'. The woman who wrote the stockpiles of letters was somebody else entirely.

She had always seemed so curt to me—at times even cold—the kind of person who could greet you with, 'You've put on weight.' When I was ten or eleven we were learning about computers at school. One night, when Shan-Yi was around for dinner, I asked if I could show her what I had been learning. With a chilly disinterest that would be burnt into my memory forever she said, 'I don't understand computers and I have no interest in them. Thank you very much.'

When I was fifteen she demanded to know why I didn't have a boyfriend yet, so I stared at my lap in silence. In her last years when her memory was on a short loop, she became obsessed with my mother's knees, exclaiming how giant and ugly they were on a ten-minute cycle. She never seemed sentimental at all to me, but her letters were full of sentiment, her written words bursting with love.

It never occurred to me that she was writing to family back home in the States about me and my brother. It felt strange to realise that she wasn't just mine, but theirs—much in the same way that it's difficult to comprehend that your parents had whole lives before you were born. It never occurred to me that people on the other side of the world might know about my birth or care who I was. But there it was in the letters, proud descriptions of my childhood milestones.

Then there were the love letters, piles and piles of them. She wrote daily to Andrew whenever he travelled—post cards, aerograms, impossibly long letters. Riffling shamelessly through her words drew out softer memories, memories of generosities I'd never even noticed. My mother, my brother, and I have consecutive birthdays—the sixteenth, seventeenth, and eighteenth of July. Each year, when we went to her place to celebrate, she'd have three beautiful heart-shaped cakes in three different flavours, our names piped across each in chocolate icing. Being the well-resourced woman that she was, it wasn't until I cleared the heart-shaped cake tin and piping bags from the kitchen that it occurred to me she had made them herself. When I showed Mum and Dad they were shocked.

It was a version of Shan-Yi that I didn't really remember, but it was a person I could imagine running away from home because she'd been inspired by Warsing, or fleeing to India to marry Karl. A person who might build a life around Andrew in Sydney, devote her life to his son and family. I had managed to make a mess out of my life by falling in love too often and too completely, I wondered if it was the same trait that made her life so satisfying. But even as the thought occurred to me I felt myself squeezing her into a box, forcing her from independent adventurer to love-struck wanderer. She wasn't the romantic or the pragmatist, she was something in between. I couldn't pin her down.

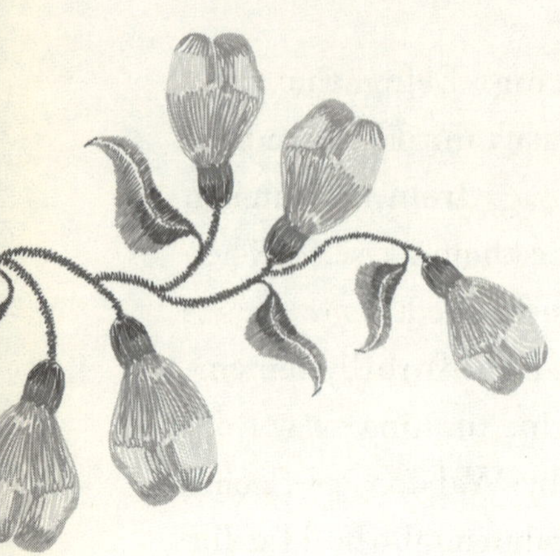

To Ninety

When Shan-Yi was in her fifties, Clare Harris, an old Idaho university friend, visited the apartment in Bellevue Hill. When Clare came down the spiral staircase that wound its way around the atrium-heart of the building, she looked up through its centre in awe. Entering the apartment she hurried over to the windows, marvelling at the harbour.

'Gee,' she said. 'I must say, you are comfortably off.'

It was an ordinary phrase, one Shan-Yi had heard a dozen times before, but something about the way that Clare spoke struck her. 'Comfortably off' were the exact words that Warsing had used as they glided away from a barren island on the Pearl River all those years ago. It had been decades since Shan-Yi had thought of the sage. She remembered the day, of course—the picture-book fortune teller, the little boy, the rickety boat, the sandbank—but she never really considered the prophecy. She wasn't a religious woman; she wasn't superstitious. She didn't believe in astrology—walking under a ladder didn't cause bad luck, when she died she would be nothing but worm food. But in that moment, standing there in the apartment with Clare, everything Warsing said came rushing back.

'You'll be married twice. Both times to Europeans, never to an Asian man. You'll have four children. You'll always be lucky in life—never rich, never poor—but in your middle years you'll be comfortably off. You'll live until you are ninety.'

She felt as though her knees were going to buckle. She grabbed the arm of the couch to steady herself, while Clare stared at her, confused.

She *had* been married twice, both times to Europeans. She *had* always been lucky in life, never rich and never poor. She was in her middle years now and she *was* very comfortably off. And then there was the other memory, the one she had pushed back into the darkest corner of her mind. The second memory to arise for the first time in a long time: the four abortions she had undergone during her years of marriage with Karl. The four children they chose not to have.

From that day on Shan-Yi believed the sage's words with absolute certainty. She would die at ninety, it had been foretold.

She was sixty-four when her grandson, Matt, finally returned to Australia in 1980, no longer a curious baby but an eighteen-year-old man. His father Albin remained in Italy with Diana and their three-year-old son Charles, living in the ancient hilltop village of Mazzano Romano, outside Rome.

Matt had visited over the years, but now he was an Australian resident, studying in Armidale at the University of New England. Shan-Yi and Andrew wrote to him and called him on the phone, but the responses they got back were usually brief, illegible scribbles written between drinking and studying for exams, smoking and mucking about with friends. They treasured them all the same.

When Matt married Carmel, the couple moved down to Sydney, much to his grandparents' delight. Matt took a job at a market-research firm and Carmel worked in biochemistry at the University of Sydney. Soon after, the country girl and the European vagabond bought a little house in Leichhardt in the Inner West. The floorboards creaked, the paint was peeling, the air smelled damp. Andrew worked himself into a panic the first time he saw it.

'We should help them buy something that isn't falling apart,' he told Shan-Yi. 'Something nearby—in Rose Bay. We need to keep them close to us.'

'Relax,' she replied. 'They'll figure it out.'

By their next visit Matt and Carmel had painted the walls and polished the floorboards. Matt had even made a stained-glass window to fill a gaping hole in the kitchen wall. Andrew was horrified to think of his untrained grandson cutting glass, but Shan-Yi thought it was pretty. Soon Matt and Carmel had two children of their own, Michelle and Tristan. And Shan-Yi earnt the title of great-grandmother. It was lovely to hold a baby again. And there were two of them now, two that wouldn't move away.

Widow

It was comforting to know Shan-Yi would live to ninety but there were holes in the prophecy, unspoken aspects—realities of her life that weren't factored in. Her sense of security was misplaced. Andrew was eighty-six when a heart attack stole him from her. His deep Hungarian voice would fill the flat no more. They'd been married forty-six years and she was in her seventies—if the prophecy was true she had fourteen years left on her own.

In the weeks after Andrew died, Shan-Yi drew the blinds and refused visitors. She had no husband to clean for, so dust gathered on the ornaments and spiders spun webs behind the curtains. She had no husband to cook for, so she didn't eat. There was no reason to do anything, no reason to live at all. Her life in Sydney was built around Andrew, he was her family on this side of the world. She felt untethered and without purpose, she felt that half of her was gone.

It took months of effort from friends and family to draw her from the shadows. Neighbours insisted on visiting and Matt and Carmel forced her across town to the Inner West for dinner. She resisted, was irritable and harsh, but as a year wore by she began to clean out the cobwebs and open the blinds one at a time. Light slowly crept back in.

Shan-Yi saw her great-grandchildren Michelle and Tristan christened and confirmed. She celebrated their birthdays, cheered them on at sports carnivals, and wrote to Albin with all the news. In 1996, Albin and Diana came to Australia with eighteen-year-old Charles to celebrate Shan-Yi's eightieth birthday. Over forty friends and family—including Cora, Bob, and their spouses, who flew in from the States—attended the big Chinese banquet in Rose Bay. Shan-Yi dressed in black and wore a big gold choker, embellished with jade and pearls. Bob gave a speech about his crazy sister Alice who ran away from home.

Three years later, Diana and Albin came for another visit. They caught trains into the city and enjoyed the winter's sunshine at Manly. Shan-Yi went with her son, her grandson, and her two great-grandchildren to explore the new Sydney Olympic site, which was still under construction. When they said their goodbyes, she encouraged Albin and Diana to come back soon—but that visit was the last time she would see her son.

In December of 2002, Albin died of lung cancer in a hospital in Rome. Diana called Shan-Yi first. Shan-Yi knew what was coming—Albin's condition had been deteriorating for months. She hung up the phone and then picked it up again, dialling Matt's number. She broke the news of his father's death quickly, but she worried about Matt—his mother Margot had died of a stomach ulcer only two years earlier.

Shan-Yi was eighty-five and when she thought about the future, it was a relief to know that her time was coming soon. She would go on to outlive her son by twelve years and her husband by twenty, but when Albin died she drew comfort from the false belief that she only had five winters left.

In the years that followed Albin's death she continued to spend time with her family, played competitive bridge at the club in Double Bay and lunched at local cafés with friends. She watched Michelle in high school musicals and watched Tristan play rugby. But over time the significant events in the children's lives seemed to grow louder than they had been before—the rooms were all more crowded. It was a strain to hear what others said, she wasn't always quite sure what was going on.

She persisted with minimal complaint—but she preferred quiet dinners, spending her time with the people she knew best. The immensity of the world had once been exciting, her belly growling with a hunger that couldn't be sated but now she felt full and tired. There was little left to long for, the boundlessness of the Earth was daunting. She drew her own life close around her.

Great-Granddaughter

I was mapping her life across great sheets of paper, linking events and characters like a detective solving a case. She lived before the digital age, leaving behind a trail of tangible files—her history was material. Letters and diaries, passports and school reports—her memories had a texture, a smell. I didn't expect to find anything online. But I thought I'd try my luck.

When I typed her name into Google, I thought the search might come up with a link to my own Facebook page, or perhaps an obituary from the local paper. But the first result was an article from the *Sydney Morning Herald*, written one month after her death, but having nothing to do with it. It was a piece about then Federal Attorney- General Nicola Roxon's expansion of government surveillance powers, entitled 'Be Careful. She Might Hear You'.

The last place I would have looked for Shan-Yi was in a series of articles dealing with online privacy. But there she was, sitting in my browser, 'Shanyi Maier, the Chinese wife of a German internee and alleged femme fatale'. It was from this article that I learnt she was the subject of the very first telephone tapping and bugging operation in the country. I knew that she had been spied on—it was family legend—but I never imagined microphones placed around her home, agents sitting in a room above her apartment, listening through headphones and transcribing her most intimate moments. Once more, I was introduced to a new version of Shan-Yi—a new path to follow along the winding course of her life.

It took months to access the surveillance files. They had to be pulled from the national archive and authorised and digitised. When I finally printed them out they formed a hefty pile—police reports, immigration files and surveillance transcripts to be sifted through. I linked the information up to all the other pieces, writing notes into spreadsheets that expanded by the day. I developed a system of colour-coding: clues from Karl's diaries and letters, Andrew's business files, personal documents of David Forbes Martyn's that had ended up in her hands. I wrote emails to her nieces and nephews in America, spoke to them via video call. I looked through old photos, matching names to faces that were previously unknown.

Four years after Shan-Yi died I found the time and money to follow in her footsteps. Mum and I flew to Hong Kong first. We looked out over the harbour, ran our fingers against lush trees, tasted local dishes and spent time at the library of the Hong Kong Museum of History. From Hong Kong we caught the train to Guangzhou, the city of skyscrapers that was once Canton. We walked through Sun Yat-Sen University, the college that was once Lingnan. In a country screeching towards the future in a race of technology and innovation, I asked local experts and tour guides to show us the 1930s.

From China, Mum headed home to Sydney and I boarded a flight to Los Angeles. It wasn't the first time I'd travelled by myself and I experienced the familiar rush of adrenaline that comes with landing in a foreign country alone. I flew on to Seattle, excited to explore the city that Shan-Yi had taken solitary walks through. Unfortunately, I landed in a country covered in snow but headed towards a boiling point, waiting on the inauguration of a president who threatened to change it all. While locals couldn't tear their eyes away from the new, I was searching for the old—placing myself in the period from presidents Monroe to Van Buren. Wandering the Seattle streets in the winter twilight, it was easy to imagine a time when the art-deco architecture and clunky old lampposts glistened with modernity. It was January and the navy-blue evenings came early, I was lost in a city of Christmas trees and golden fairy lights. I stayed back in the library after dark, examining maps and reading newspapers stored on microfilm. One night, on the way back to my hostel, I looked up at the painted awning of the Fifth Avenue Theatre and wondered if this was what it felt like to step into a picture book.

*

I ate clam chowder and drank local beers, tasted salmon at the Pike Place Markets. I wandered through the lobbies of heritage hotels, searching for the mezzanine from which Shan-Yi first saw Donald. Mum was horrified at the idea of my driving in the snow, so I caught the bus across Washington state, winding through the mountains and the flat centre just like Shan-Yi had. In Ellensburg, I walked a mile along the open road from the Holiday Inn to Main Street, snow falling all around me. While locals sat cosy in their homes and enjoyed the Christmas break, I spent days trudging through the snow in gumboots, my bare hand suspended in the air while I took photos with my phone.

A woman approached me in the supermarket, where I was walking aimlessly down the aisles to take a break from the cold.

'Can I ask where you bought those boots?' she said. 'My daughter is a freshman and I want to buy her some like yours. We keep seeing you out in the street—you look so warm!'

I was excited to have someone to chat to and proud that my bitter expedition had been noticed but I politely explained that I was the last person she should ask for tips on surviving the frosty Pacific Northwest.

In Moscow, Idaho, I visited the old family business. There was still a restaurant in its place—a recent addition to the town, serving hearty seasonal lunches made from local ingredients. The restaurant was new, but the old wooden booths remained—'The Grill' written above the counter in aged gold letters. Over a cosy bowl of carrot soup, I told the new owners about my family. They knew the whole story—Yee and the snack, the impulse purchase—as they'd read about it in the local paper just a couple of years ago.

The librarian at Moscow High invited me in with a broad Idaho grin, as though the White-Australian step-great-grandchild of a Chinese-born graduate from 1932 happened by every day. We walked together down halls lined with lockers, like the set from every American teen TV show. The mascot's red bear paw prints lined the walls. She took me into a storeroom and pulled out piles of old school newspapers, sifting through to Alice Lee's time. I spent hours sitting in the library while a class took place around me, taking picture after picture of her name in print while teenagers passed by unperturbed.

At local historical societies and libraries from Idaho to Washington, I became a student of street directories and town plans—examining 1920s cartography and cross-referencing with Google Maps to figure out where she'd been. I walked her route in Moscow from the café to school and home again, strolled along Greek-row at the University of Idaho, looked up at a framed photograph of Professor Carl Claus.

I arrived back in Sydney with a new idea of Shan-Yi's life. My research had grown exponentially, my luggage was heavy with history books and photocopies and filled-up notepads. Then there were the other souvenirs—the tastes and the smells and the low-hanging sun—the memories of my own. I had so much more than I ever imagined, but I still wasn't ready. I didn't feel confident, there were still questions left. I was waiting for that decisive moment when I would feel that I had her all figured out. A moment of clarity and self-assuredness. It took a lot of time and exhausted leads to realise that that moment was never coming. There would *always* be questions left. I would *always* want to know more. I could only have the version of Shan-Yi that existed in my mind—a story filled in by my own thoughts and experiences, threaded together with the recorded facts. It was the version of her life that could be pieced together from what she left behind and my imagination. As for the facts that went *un*recorded—the whispered words and fleeting daydreams—those were gone. Forgotten.

I wasn't a writer. Not exactly. I wasn't being paid. I wasn't a journalist either, not a producer, or a beauty blogger, or an Instagram starlet. I would probably never be invited to Fashion Week again. I wasn't anyone's girlfriend and I didn't expect to be anytime soon. But each day I got up, and each night I went to bed. I had food in my belly and a roof over my head. I had something to write, a story to tell—a story that nobody else would tell. She was lifting me up all over again. Shan-Yi kept pulling me out of the darkness.

Sometimes I worried what it would be like once I finished writing her story—if I'd somehow know what to do next. Without a project in hand would I go slipping back into the corners of my mind? But the truth was, it didn't matter. I would *always* have to work towards feeling ok. Now, I had proof that I could pick myself up—I knew what I needed to get through the day. Friendship and family, exercise, financial security to pay the bills, a chance to use my imagination. I couldn't take credit for the rarefied opportunity to live in Shan-Yi's home; but I had taken that opportunity and kept going. I could keep going again.

That was what she had done really, over and over in her

life—picked up at each hurdle and just carried on. Perhaps she wasn't more confident than I was at all, perhaps she just chose not to fret about the past. She made the choices she had to make to get by, and then charged on wherever they led. She didn't look back, didn't grieve for the path she started out on. Maybe that simple fact was the very answer I wanted from her—just make a choice and go on. She didn't have time for any other way.

Everywhere and Nowhere

Gradually, Shan-Yi's memory failed her. She didn't know how long she had been home, didn't know where she was going. She couldn't answer questions, didn't know what to say. She was well past ninety now, but she couldn't remember her precise age. She knew her great-granddaughter's face, but she couldn't remember her name. She was still the consummate salesperson, ever the charming hostess. When strangers came and sat in her bedroom, she never asked 'Who are you?' but 'How are you?' She made polite conversation as they stroked her forehead, continued to chat though her words turned back on her and melted away. She was gracious and accommodating, she listened and nodded along.

The heater in her bedroom ran day and night, casting orange light through the gloom. Her world was a tangle of sheets and blankets, her legs were wrapped in bandages, her feet covered in sores. She was sinking into the bed, she wished it would swallow her whole. She wanted to fall into its depths—she wanted to be one with the blankets. She was ready to disappear, to be part of the warmth.

The day she left the apartment, strange men came to carry her away. They took her to the palliative care ward; the hospital was stark in its whiteness. She could feel metal against her feet, lights shone in her eyes. Faces hovered above her—familiar ones and foreign ones, young ones and old. She squinted and reached her arms about, seeking something to hold on to.

She knew this bed; she knew this place. She was in her bedroom in Moscow, sitting by the fireplace of the Bergonian Hotel. She was sculling along in a sampan, waiting for her father to return to the car. She could smell dried tangerine peel and musty paper, the pungent polish she rubbed on her violin. There was ink all over her fingers, ink from every letter that she had ever written. Andrew was holding her hand; her mother was calling her name. She was everywhere and nowhere. And then she was gone.

Author's Note

Yee Lee walked into Huff's Café to buy a snack and came out having bought the restaurant. That part of the story is agreed upon by all. But Marie remembered only Cora and her mother being there, after having spent the day exploring the Palouse with the intention of returning to Spokane. By contrast, Shan-Yi insisted she was there too. She said the stop in Moscow was made by the whole family—that she waited in the car with her mother and two sisters en route to New York from Spokane, headed out of the Pacific Northwest.

I found many discrepancies like this while researching Shan-Yi's life. My purpose has been to tell her story, and so I have taken a 'Shan-Yi first' approach to resolving such challenges—fact-checking her claims but in cases of uncertainty placing her memories before those of others. In the case of her divorce from Karl, the letters between the pair were full of conflicting accusations. By comparing their correspondence with Shan-Yi's filmed account, I have tried to unearth the truth. That said, there have been blanks and I have shared Shan-Yi's experience, not Karl's.

I was surprised how mundane many of my sources were. I consulted shipping manifests, street directories, census data, and other dense statistical documents to plot the points of Shan-Yi's life and match recollections to specific places and dates. The time I spent travelling or hunkered down in libraries helped me to see her in more detail, but in the end this story draws most heavily on three primary sources—a video of Shan-Yi recounting her memories; her correspondence; and a four-part oral history recorded by Marie Lee Lew and Mi Lew for the Latah County Historical Society. These sources provided me with access to Shan-Yi's life in ways that no book, museum, or expert ever could.

There are two points for which there is scant information. The first was her quarrel with the dean of women at Lingnan University. There is no record of this beyond the details that I've shared. The second was in regard to Shan-Yi's extra-marital affairs. When she wrote to Karl that their marriage was over, he accused her of leaving him for another man. She vehemently denied this, although her letters to Andrew confirmed they were already in a relationship. While she denied this second affair, Karl and Shan-Yi agreed she had strayed earlier. She shared the reasons she was attracted to the man she had a relationship with, and it is clear that she confessed the affair to Karl shortly after it occurred. I don't know the identity of this man or the details of their relationship. I have combined her memories of life in

Sydney during the 1940s with her few references to the affair to create my best approximation of what happened.

On the shipping record for the *Empress of Russia*, Shan-Yi's name is spelled 'Jim Yee', elsewhere I have seen it spelled 'Jung Yee'. 'Shan-Yi' is the spelling that she chose as an adult, and for clarity is the only spelling that I have chosen to use. After she discarded the name 'Alys' she wrote to Warsing, 'I also have changed my name, to "Shan-Yi", rather naively, I think. It is not Mandarin, or Cantonese, or anything on earth, but my friends like it.' She liked the way her name looked at the bottom of a letter, signed with a great flourish of the 'S'—she liked to be called 'Shan' by those who loved her.

In rare cases, I have given fictitious names to her unnamed acquaintances. In the cases of present-day businesses, colleagues, and acquaintances in my life, names have been changed for the purpose of preserving privacy.

The United States and Australia share a long history of discrimination against Asian immigrants. During the 1920s, when Shan-Yi arrived in America, the *Chinese Exclusion Act*, renewed as the *Geary Act*, limited Chinese immigration and placed onerous restrictions on Chinese residents. The *United States Immigration Act* of 1924 banned most immigration from Asia. In 1927, when Shan-Yi was eleven, the US Supreme court found that states had the right to define a Chinese student as non-white for the purpose of racial segregation in public schools, although this was not implemented in Moscow, Idaho.

When Shan-Yi arrived in Australia with Karl, the 'White Australia Policy' was in full force. While the policy was dismantled in 1973, the change did little to end cultural and institutional discrimination against Asian Australians. In 1996, when Shan-Yi turned eighty, Pauline Hanson was elected to the Australian House of Representatives on a platform of anti-Asian rhetoric.

In many ways, Shan-Yi's life was a privileged one. Her wealth and circumstances shielded her from many of the obstacles that Asian Americans and Asian Australians face. I cannot personally speak to the experience of living as a racial minority and it has not been my intention to do so in this book. In order to tell Shan-Yi's story with honesty, I have described her experience as closely to her own words as possible. The experiences of immigrants are rich and diverse. This is the experience of one woman, who lived a unique life, culturally and physically distanced from her biological family.

I have, at different stages of my life, been diagnosed with clinical depression, an anxiety disorder, Obsessive Compulsive Disorder, and Bipolar Disorder. I chose to include my experiences between the years of 2012 and 2015, a period during which I lived with severe depression. I have seen psychologists since I was a child. Some made me feel that therapy was useless while others improved my quality of life to varying degrees. In 2012, I was fortunate to find a psychologist who I trust implicitly. I have been seeing her for seven years. I have been taking medication to assist with my mental health for eight years. Exercise has been an essential part of my recovery. I am not a natural athlete, but have come to realise that exercise does as much for the mind as it does for the body, and I need my mind in order. Nowadays I run as regularly as I can, even though I often don't want to. If you are experiencing depression, anxiety, or dealing with a personal crisis of any kind, Lifeline provides 24-hour personal crisis support by phone and text. For twelve to twenty-five-year olds, Headspace centres across Australia provide mental healthcare, including both online and telephone support services.

When Shan-Yi was cremated in 2012, we scattered her ashes over the garden below her apartment in Bellevue Hill. It was the same spot over which Andrew's ashes were scattered twenty years earlier. That was where she wanted to rest—she didn't want a funeral. Sometimes I drive down Drumalbyn Road, where I lived for just over eighteen months and she lived for more than sixty-seven years. I pull over to the side of the road, get out and walk by her building. If you pass the driveway, you can see the harbour stretched out beyond the white art-deco building that stands tall like a lighthouse, looking down from above. That's where she lives on the salty sea breeze, where I feel her crumpled cheek against mine. I go there to be in the place she chose—to be in the place we shared.

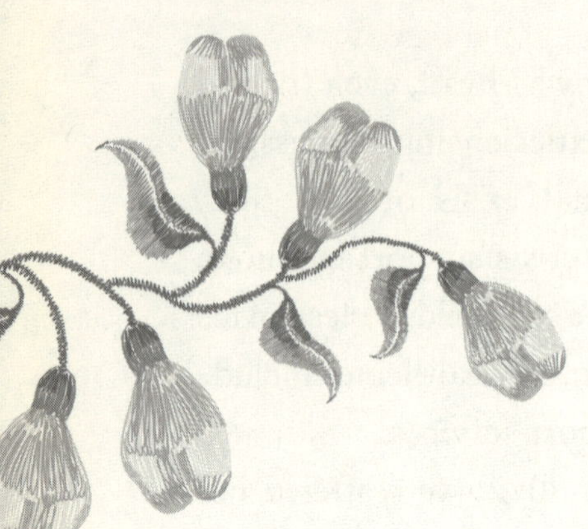

Acknowledgements

This book was made possible by my family. I was privileged to meet Shan-Yi's siblings Marie, Cora and Bob when I was a child, but the original Moscow Lees are no longer with us—it was their descendants who kindly answered my questions and offered me help with this book. To the many Lees, Lews, Aus and more who are part of my extended family, I hope this book does justice to the lives that inspired it. To those who spoke to me over phone, skype, and email—thank you for your generosity. Shan-Yi spent most of her life forging her path away from the family and I hope this book brings a little of her back home.

My mum shifted to part-time work in order to provide care for Shan-Yi during her final years. At the same time, Mum managed to provide patient love and care for a daughter suffering from severe depression—unsurprising given the constant support she has offered me throughout my life. Thank you to Mum, Dad and Tristan, who've lived through the hard times and the amazing times, who loved Shan-Yi and loved me and gave me free reign to tell this story.

Thank you to the extended Balogh/Loblay family and especially to Andrew's nephew Lorand who, at ninety-five, sat down with me to answer hours of questions. Thanks also to an adopted member of the family, Shan-Yi's cleaner-turned-carer, Sara Alvarez, who soaked my grandmother's sore feet, filled her belly, eased her fears and showed a level of devotion for which I could never be grateful enough.

My twenties, a portion of which are chronicled in this book, taught me the value of steadfast friends. I'd like to thank Amy, Elyse, Jake, Jo, Loretta and Sarah, each of whom were supporters and early readers, but who made me the kind of person who could write this book.

Thank you to the staff at 169 Darlinghurst for the coffee, wine, chat, working space and time to write this story.

To my psychologist, Tash. I am a writer because I have help—your help these last seven years has been arguably the most important step towards making this book a reality.

Beyond family and friends and therapists, it took many hands to do this work. During my travels abroad, there were many people and places that contributed to my understanding of Shan-Yi's life. In particular, Seattle's Wing Luke Museum of the Asian Pacific American Experience, the Latah County Historical Society and Moscow High School were sources of invaluable information.

Thank you to Aviva Tuffield whose faith first made me believe that my short story could be a novel. My agents at Cameron's, Jo Butler and Jeanne Ryckmans, who each provided wisdom, encouragement and kindness, shoring me through many moments of self doubt. My editor, Alice Grundy, who stuck by me through this long and winding process, providing necessary discernment and valuable insight. Jing Han who provided a sensitivity read, without which a story like this could not exist. The team at Brio Books who chose to back my book, believed in both me and Shan-Yi, and saw this project through to the shelf.

Finally and most importantly, thank you to Shan-Yi. The woman who thought it was silly to worry over the dead but who has managed to fill my mind every day since she's been gone. My inspiration, my grandmother. I hope I've done you justice.